NEAL-SCHUMAN

AUTHORITATIVE GUIDE TO EVALUATING INFORMATION ON THE INTERNET

ALISON COOKE

NEAL-SCHUMAN NETGUIDE SERIES

NEAL-SCHUMAN PUBLISHERS, INC.

NEW YORK   LONDON

Published by
Neal-Schuman Publishers, Inc.
100 Varick Street
New York, NY 10013

Printed and bound in the United States of America.

Library of Congress Cataloging-in-Publication Data

Cooke, Alison,
     Neal-Schuman authoritative guide to evaluating information on the
Internet / Alison Cooke.
          p.   cm. — (Neal-Schuman NetGuide series)
     Includes bibliographical references (p.   ) and index.
     ISBN 1-55570-356-9
     1. Computer network resources—Evaluation. 2. Computer network
resources—United States—Evaluation. I. Title. II. Title:
Authoritative guide to evaluating information on the Internet.
III. Series: Neal Schuman net-guide series.
     ZA4201.C66   1999
          025.04—dc21   99-28010
                                                                                      CIP

ISBN 1-55570-356-9

Published in cooperation with the Library Association, London.

Contents

Acknowledgments

I would like to thank the Department of Information and Library Studies, University of Wales Aberystwyth, where I validated the evaluation criteria included in this book over a four-year period. I interviewed hundreds of Internet users concerning a specific case when they had used the Internet to look for information, and the interview transcripts were analyzed to determine how assessments of quality were made and to identify evaluation criteria. The results were developed into a tool for assessing the quality of Internet-based information sources; this was distributed to library and information professionals for review. A second stage of interviewing was also undertaken to validate the initial findings. A final version of the tool was developed, based upon the results of the second interviews and the comments and criticisms received from the library and information professionals involved in the reviewing process. Chapters 3 and 4 of this book are largely based upon this tool.

I would like to express my sincere gratitude to the *OMNI Project Board* for their support throughout the research which formed the basis of this book, and in particular to Betsy Anagnostelis (Deputy Librarian, Medical Library, Royal Free and University College Medical School of University College of London [UCL]) for her unending enthusiasm and assistance. In addition, I am grateful to Frank Norman (National Institute for Medical Research) and Sue Welsh (also previously at the National Institute for Medical Research), Bob Parkinson (Queen's Medical Centre, Nottingham University), and Wendy Roberts (School of Clinical Medicine, Cambridge University) for their help and assistance in arranging the fieldwork. I would like to thank all those who participated in the fieldwork for their time and cooperation, and all the information professionals who offered advice and feedback at various stages throughout the research. I would also like to express my gratitude to the University of Wales for funding the research, and to the members of staff at the Department of Information and Library Studies, University of Wales, Aberystwyth, and in particular my Ph.D supervisors, David Stoker and Su James, for their professional support and advice.

I would also like to acknowledge and express my gratitude to the *OMNI Advisory Group for Evaluation Criteria.* It was work with Betsy Anagnostelis (Deputy Librarian, Medical Library, Royal Free and University College Medical School of UCL) and Alison McNab (Academic Services Manager, Pilkington Library, Loughborough University) through this group which shaped much of the thinking behind Chapter 2.

Preface

I have written the *Neal-Schuman Authoritative Guide to Evaluating Information on the Internet* because although the Internet can sometimes prove to be a valuable source of information, it can also be a frustrating waste of time and the information which is available is often useless, outdated, or difficult to authenticate.

The *Authoritative Guide to Evaluating Information on the Internet* is a comprehensive tool, designed to assist Internet users in:

■ searching for quality information sources available via the Internet
■ assessing the quality of materials once they have found them.

The book is divided into the following sections:

■ the Internet and information quality
■ using search facilities to maximize quality information retrieval
■ assessing the quality of any Internet information source
■ evaluating particular types of sources
■ an annotated bibliography
■ a glossary.

The Internet and information quality

Chapter 1 provides an introduction and background to the concept of quality in relation to the information available via the Internet. It contains some examples of problems relating to the quality of this information, followed by a brief overview of how those problems arose. The terms "information quality" and "information source" are then defined, and the role of the book in assessing information quality is considered in order to provide a framework and point of reference for the book as a whole.

Using search facilities to maximize quality information retrieval

There is an ever-increasing range of tools and facilities which enable users to search for information available via the Internet and the World Wide Web (WWW). These range from general search engines such as *Lycos* or *AltaVista*, through general subject directories such as *Yahoo!* and rating services such as *Lycos Top 5%*, to services for accessing high-quality materials, such as the Internet Public Library. This section provides a guide to the different types of search facilities which are now available, a description of some examples (including those mentioned here) and how they work, their respective advantages and disadvantages, and what to use when attempting to find high-quality materials. The aim of this chapter is to introduce readers to the wider range of search facilities which are now available, and to provide some suggestions on how to look for useful materials.

Assessing the quality of any Internet information source

Chapter 3 focuses on assessing quality. It is divided into ten areas of evaluation (e.g., accuracy, currency, ease of use), which require consideration in the evaluation of any information source available via the Internet. Each section contains extensive notes on how to approach the particular aspect of evaluation, and there is a checklist for quick reference.

Evaluating particular types of sources

A wide range of different types of information sources is now available via the Internet. Examples include personal WWW home pages, organizational sites, Usenet newsgroups, FTP archives, electronic journals – the list is almost endless. Different people access and use these different sources for different reasons, and may be interested in different quality issues. For example, a user of a personal home page might be more concerned with the authority of the information, while a user of a File Transfer Protocol (FTP) archive might wish to assess access speeds. Therefore, Chapter 4 is concerned with evaluating different types of information sources. Each section includes criteria which are specific to each source type, with detailed notes on their application and use. A checklist for each source type is also included for easy referral.

Annotated bibliography and glossary

The final part of the book is an annotated bibliography of other guidelines which are available for selecting and evaluating Internet-based information sources. A glossary of relevant terms is also included.

Who should use the guide, and when?

Anyone, anywhere, anyhow . . .

Ultimately, the *Authoritative Guide to Evaluating Information on the Internet* is aimed at any user of the Internet, and the number of potential situations in which an Internet user might want to assess the quality of a source is almost infinite. One reader might need to conduct a search relating to a project and want to know the best places to start looking. Another, who needs an answer to a specific question, might have identified some potentially relevant sources and needs to establish the accuracy and reliability of the information he or she has found. The guide offers indicators of where to start looking for information, and how to make a quality assessment when potentially relevant materials have been located.

The guide will be especially helpful to those who are new to using the Internet or who are less experienced in evaluating the quality of information sources, as it provides an introduction to searching the Internet and a thorough grounding in assessing quality. It will also be of value to experienced evaluators and Internet users, as it provides ideas on searching for quality sources of information, a reminder of the different issues requiring consideration in source evaluation, and pointers towards an extensive range of further relevant materials.

Library and information professionals

Library professionals who are involved in the selection and evaluation of Internet-based information sources will find this guide advantageous. It can be used as a reference manual for selecting resources for inclusion in library collections. In addition, it might be used for training or advising library users on how to assess the quality of information available via the Internet, and in order to increase awareness of the need to think critically about sources of information generally.

Developers of Internet materials

The guide will assist WWW page authors and developers of other Internet sources when producing and maintaining their materials. It might be used to select other sources to link to for further information – site developers might wish to assess the currency of a source in order to determine whether its material will quickly become outdated and thus not be worth linking to. In addition, site developers might want to assess the quality of their own materials. The guide could be used to highlight options for improving the quality of materials, or to provide hints to enable external users to assess the quality of a site.

How should the guide be used?

Newcomers to the Internet and to evaluation

Newcomers both to the Internet and to evaluating sources of information are advised to work systematically through the book. New users should begin by reading Chapter 1, "The Internet and Information Quality," which introduces the concept of quality in relation to information available on the Internet. Chapter 2, on "Using Search Facilities to Maximize Quality Information Retrieval," should then be examined as it explains the variations between different search facilities and provides numerous tips on how to search the Internet more effectively. Readers are advised to then read "Assessing the Quality of Any Internet Information Source," in order to become familiar with source assessment. By reading through Chapter 3 in its entirety, readers will be provided with a thorough grounding in the various factors affecting the quality of any information source which can be accessed via the Internet.

When seeking high-quality materials

Chapter 2, on "Using Search Facilities to Maximize Quality Information Retrieval," provides a guide to the different types of search facilities which are now available, some examples of each, how they work, their respective advantages and disadvantages, and how they can be used to look for high-quality materials. The chapter provides guidelines on where to start looking, as well as ideas for finding high-quality sources.

When assessing a specific source

Many readers will want to evaluate a particular type of source, and for them the most relevant section is Chapter 4 on "Evaluating Particular Types of Sources." First, readers in this position should decide what type of information source they have (for example, a personal WWW home page? A Usenet newsgroup? An electronic journal?). In many cases, this will be immediately obvious from the source itself, but readers may want to examine the definitions of the different source types. Once readers have decided which source type they want to evaluate, they should then examine the relevant section.

If readers are unable to decide on a particular source type, Chapter 3 on "assessing quality" is applicable to the evaluation of any source available on the Internet. Moreover, many of the issues discussed in Chapter 3 are also applicable to the specific source types. In order to prevent repetition, these discussions have not been repeated in Chapter 4, but readers are referred back to the appropriate sections.

Expert Internet users and evaluators

Users who are familiar with using the Internet and with evaluating different types of information sources may find they can begin immediately with the checklists provided at the end of each section for assessing quality, and at the end of the sections relating to each source type. These will provide a valuable reminder of what to look for when assessing quality. Other users may find it beneficial to refer initially to the detailed explanatory notes, but to use the checklists as they become more familiar with source assessment.

1
The Internet and Information Quality

The purpose of this chapter is to provide the reader with background information about problems relating to the quality of Internet-based information sources, an awareness of the process of quality assessment, and an understanding of how this book fits into that process.

Some examples of the types of problems relating to information available via the Internet are examined, namely:

- information overload
- the availability of vast quantities of useless information
- the potential for inaccurate materials
- the ephemeral nature of materials disseminated via personal home pages.

The development of the Internet generally, and the World Wide Web (WWW) in particular, are then discussed in order to provide some explanation of why such problems have arisen.

The terms "information quality" and "information source" are defined in order to develop an understanding of what is meant by a "quality information source." These terms are referred to throughout the book and it is essential that they are defined in order to provide a point of reference for the book as a whole. Finally, the role of the book in assessing information quality is considered in order to establish a framework for the reader.

What are the problems with information on the Internet?

In 1969, the beginnings of "the Internet" consisted of four networked computers located in three universities and a research institute in America. By the early 1980s, that number had grown to over 1,000, and by January 1999 over 43,230,000 host computers distributed throughout almost every continent and country across the globe were connected to the Internet.[1] Advances in computer networking during the 1990s offered unforeseen advantages in terms of accessing and disseminating information, and the resulting explosion in the volume and variety of sources could never have been predicted. The number of Usenet newsgroups multiplied from three in 1979, to 10,696 in 1994, and the number of WWW sites from 133 in 1993, to 10,022 at the end of 1994. By March 1999, there were some 4,389,131 WWW sites.[1] However, the rapid explosion in resources also brought with it many problems for Internet users.

Too much of a good thing

The ease of publishing via the Internet has resulted in users being increasingly faced with an unimaginable quantity and variety of sources of potential interest to them. The problem has been further compounded by a lack of sophisticated search tools. Many search facilities have remained limited in their capabilities and are consequently not adequate to deal with the volume of available resources. Search engines such as *Excite* (**http://www.excite.com/**) often return an unwieldy number of results to users' queries, and the details provided in the search output often lack enough detail to enable users to assess the relevance of the sites which are listed.

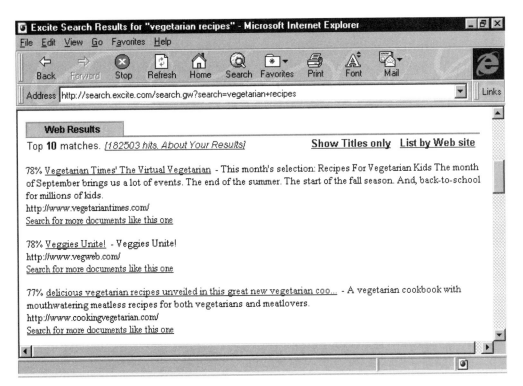

Fig. 1.1 *The results of a search for vegetarian recipes on Excite*

A seemingly straightforward search on *Excite* for "vegetarian recipes" results in 182,503 hits, as displayed in Figure 1.1, including various sites in the first ten hits which define themselves as "official" or "comprehensive." Ironically, any attempts to restrict the search, such as by adding the term "casseroles," slightly increases the number of hits – 185,492 sites are retrieved. The volume of materials retrieved, and the lack of descriptive information about them, means that the Internet can be an inefficient and time-consuming option when looking for information. Furthermore, a search result of over 180,000 sites does not necessarily mean that any of these sites will be of interest to the frustrated searcher!

Useless information

> The Internet is frequently described by its users as "a realm of pure mind." Anything which is thinkable can be expressed to an audience of hundreds of thousands.[2]

> On the Net, anyone with a computer can be his own reporter, editor, and publisher – spreading news and views to millions of readers around the world.[3]

Users are not only faced with problems of information overload. Without the constraints previously imposed by commercial and academic publishers, huge volumes of junk and material of an ephemeral nature are being produced. Simply accessing the *Useless Pages* directory (**http://www.go2net.com/internet/useless/**) provides an insight into the range of resources of questionable usefulness and value which are currently available.

As can be seen in Figure 1.2, one site of the week on the *Useless Pages* was "Real potbellied pig sounds from the jingle bellies Christmas album" (**http://www.rjbmusic.com/rjbmusic/pigwavs.htm**). A previous site of the week was "Ugly People of the Internet" (**http://www.tqci.net/~tvc15/ugly/main.html**), a collection of images of "ugly people" collated through "reader submission." It is difficult to envisage many situations in which such sites could be considered of value.

Inaccurate information

The questionable accuracy and reliability of networked information has become an issue of increasing concern. In 1996, the *British Medical Journal* noted a growth in the number of unverified health claims being made via the Internet. Examples included:

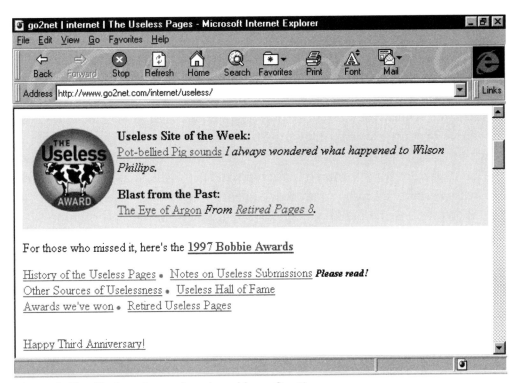

Fig. 1.2 *The Useless Pages (produced by go2net)*

Advertisements for shark cartilage which "inhibits tumour growth and cancer" and melatonin which is banned in the United Kingdom but freely available in the United States and is claimed to "strengthen the body's immune system."[4]

A review of resources on advice to deal with fever in children at home was also later published in the *British Medical Journal*.[5] Over 40 WWW pages were evaluated and compared with published guidelines, and only four provided advice which adhered closely to the published recommendations. Thus users of the Internet, including consumers of health information, are faced with attempting to detect inaccurate sources of medical advice, as well as inaccurate information generally. Users may lack the knowledge and skills to make an assessment of accuracy, or may unknowingly encounter inaccurate information from a seemingly legitimate site. Furthermore, it is not uncommon to find sites which lack any detail about the organization or individual responsible for producing the information. In such circumstances, it is difficult to ascertain the knowledge and expertise of those responsible, and therefore to assess the likely accuracy and reliability of the information.

Personal home pages

Further drawbacks relate to personal WWW home pages. Sites often contain little more than images captioned "These are my friends," "This is my cat," and "This is where I live." Additional problems arise because individuals develop a personal site while in a particular job, or while at college or a university, but after three or four years they may move on without removing the information, or without notifying external sites which point to their documents. The innocent user searches for information, attempts to follow the links from the results of a search facility or from another document, only to find "file not found" or else an incomplete and outdated page of potentially irrelevant information.

Figure 1.3 displays an example of a student's personal home page. The site provides images and information about the author, his hobbies and interests, and links to photographs of his friends with text describing them and their personal hobbies and interests. Again, it is difficult to envisage that this site will appeal to a wide audience. Following some of the links from this site results in the familiar "file not found" scenario, as some friends' pages have evidently been removed, but the links have not been updated accordingly. Indeed, "file not found" has become known as the most heavily accessed page on the

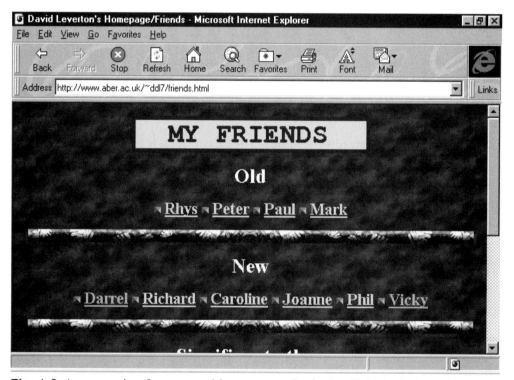

Fig. 1.3 *An example of a personal home page displaying links to information about friends and their pictures*

WWW, and almost every Internet user will have encountered links to pages that no longer exist. Others will have experienced outdated information from a seemingly reputable organization or individual, and sites which look interesting but lack any real information.

Why have these problems arisen?

The previous section has highlighted just a few of the problems associated with using the Internet to look for information. So, why have these problems arisen?

Early development of the Internet

Prior to the 1980s, Internet users had access to three basic tools: e-mail, Telnet, and File Transfer Protocol (FTP). These provided a gateway into vast quantities of information but relied upon prior knowledge of the location and availability of the resources, as well as knowledge of the commands to access and use them. Therefore, they were limited to users with some basic knowledge of computer networking, and uptake was slow.

In the late 1980s and early 1990s, the development of distributed client–server computing fundamentally altered the way in which information could be accessed via the Internet. Distributed client–server computing enables users to access information with their own local computer, the *client*, handling interaction with a remote computer, the *server*. Simply, the information is located on a remote machine, while the software for accessing the information is located on the user's machine. This enables users to make their own decisions about how they access and manipulate information. Gopher was an early example of a distributed client–server tool which offered a menu-based interface to Internet sources. The software was friendlier and more helpful than the command-line interfaces used for accessing Telnet or FTP, and individuals could browse through the menus of resources without having to know filenames and locations.

The World Wide Web and multimedia browsers

The WWW is another example of a distributed client–server tool which is built around a standard hypertext language, the HyperText Mark-up Language (HTML). HTML can be read by almost any computer system and allows users to create links between text, images, and sound files. However, early versions of WWW browsers were text-based and consequently offered few advantages over other tools. It was not until the development and free distribution of multimedia browsers for accessing the WWW, such as *Mosaic* and *Netscape Navigator*, that the potential of the Internet for information access and dissemination was fully realized. Using *Mosaic* or *Netscape*, files could be located, retrieved, and displayed easily with fully integrated text, graphics, and sound. In addition, browsers provided access, not only to WWW information in hypertext format, but also to other information sources such as Usenet newsgroups, Gopher resources, and FTP archives. Furthermore, hypertext links were quickly supplemented by subject-based catalogs and search tools, improving the ease with which users could search for and retrieve information.

An information explosion

During the 1990s, the WWW quickly became the most heavily used tool for accessing information via the Internet and there was a rapid explosion in the volume of materials which were being made available. Reasons for this included the ease of using multimedia browsers to access and generate information, as well as the benefits of producing documents in HTML. HTML initially appears confusing to the new user, but the code of existing HTML documents can be examined in order to understand how to create new sites and pages. In addition, during the 1990s a number of software packages have been developed which enable users easily to create pages without any in-depth knowledge of HTML. Many word-processing and desktop publishing (DTP) packages can now save documents in HTML format, enabling an almost instantaneous conversion of any electronic document into a format suitable for publication via the WWW.

Since its inception, the Internet has been characterized by its anarchic nature. There is no centralized control of the information it provides access to, and therefore, with the introduction and free distribution of multimedia browsers, anyone with access to the requisite hardware and software could become an author and a publisher. Budding writers were no longer constrained by the demands of commercial publishers, or by editors and referees in the academic publishing sphere. Moreover, the falling price of PCs and computer equipment generally meant that those outside academia were also able to produce information easily and cheaply. Indeed, one of the significant changes to the Internet has been a cultural shift from an academic network towards increased commercialization. In May 1995, the US government ceased to fund the Internet backbone and a number of major commercial network providers adopted the role. In addition, commercial providers such as *CompuServe*, *America Online*, and *Prodigy* began to provide Internet access through their services. Increasing commercialization of the Internet resulted in a much more varied audience and a much greater range of information sources designed to meet their needs.

What is meant by a "quality information source"?

"Information source" and "information quality" are referred to throughout the book and it is essential that these concepts are defined in order to provide a framework and point of reference for the book as a whole.

Definition of an "information source"

Information is available to people in many different forms and may be absorbed through all the senses. While walking down the street, a vast amount of information is available to everyone – from a billboard poster, to a smell from a shop, to an overheard conversation. Simply seeing a bus approaching will provide information to a passerby. As a consequence, the term "information" is used in a wide range of situations and its meaning in everyday use is often assumed rather than clearly defined.

In order to develop an understanding of what is meant by "information," commentators have attempted to draw distinctions between data, information and knowledge. For example, *data* has been defined as "a result of direct observations of events, i.e., values of attributes of objects," and *information* as "structured collections of data."[6] The respective roles of data and information have also been defined in relation to decision making: information is "data of value in decision making," which has the potential "to transform a state of knowledge."[7] In other words, data might refer to a statistic in a table of statistics. That data becomes information only if it is of potential value and has the potential to impact upon an individual's knowledge. As used in this book, information refers to any structured data sent over the Internet which has the potential to transform or alter an individual's state of knowledge.

"Information source" is generally used to refer to information which has been written down or recorded in some form for future use – books, newspaper articles, and videocassettes are all information sources. However, defining an information source in an electronic environment is problematic because of the potential to continuously change or delete information. For example, a database or an active discussion list might be referred to as an information source, but the information contained in the database or available via a discussion list may change or may be available for a short period of time only. Furthermore, electronic information sources are problematic because different levels of access are often available. A whole database may be referred to as an information source, as might an individual record in the database, and a Usenet newsgroup is in itself a source of information, as is an individual message to the group.

Within this book, "information source" is used to refer to any information which has been recorded and is available for access at the time of use. Thus, a database or a Usenet newsgroup is referred to as an information source because it provides access to information at the time of use. Furthermore, an information source is referred to as such whether it is a two-line Usenet newsgroup posting or a complete newsgroup.

Definition of "information quality"

The term "quality," like "information," is used in a wide range of contexts and its meaning is often assumed rather than clearly defined. The term is often used to denote "good quality" or "high quality" – the *Concise Oxford Dictionary* defines quality as "the degree of excellence of a thing." However, the interpretation of quality as an abstract concept of excellence is insufficient when a working definition is required.

The British Standards Institution (BSI) defines quality as "the totality of characteristics of an entity that bear on its ability to satisfy stated and implied needs."[8] In the light of this statement, it is possible to interpret quality as the ability of a product or service to meet the needs of a particular user or group of users. In this sense there is no absolute measure of quality, because what makes for a quality product or service will depend upon the needs of those concerned. However, there are characteristics of a product or service which will affect its ability to meet those needs, such as whether a service is efficient or whether a product is hard-wearing. It is these factors which can be examined in a particular situation or context to make a quality assessment.

In relation to information available via the Internet, quality is often used to refer to sources which contain original content, or sources which are accurate and reliable. Definitions of information quality have been debated on one discussion list and some of the results developed into a file of definitions.[9] Factors discussed include the usefulness of a source, the ability of a source to "get the message across," and the "level of noise" in a source. However, one participant suggests that "a Website's quality is directly proportional to its effectiveness in fulfilling the purposes for which it was intended" and "the definition must lie somewhere in the interaction between what the Website designers intended and how users respond."

This last definition is analogous to the BSI definition of quality because it avoids an absolute measure of quality. Instead, information quality refers to the fitness for its purpose of an information source within a particular setting. There can be no definitive determination of what is a quality source of information because there are so many possible variables involved, particularly in an electronic environment where the providers and users of information are likely to be numerous. However, as with a product or a service, an information source can be evaluated to determine the extent to which it meets the needs of a user, and therefore the extent to which it is of higher or lower quality within that particular context.

How can this book be used to assess information quality?

At this point it may be useful to recap and summarize. Within the context of this book, an information source refers to any information which has been recorded and is available for access at the time of use. The information contained in a source may change, and there may be different levels of access to the information. Information quality refers to the ability of an information source to meet the needs of a user. There can be no definitive determination of a quality information source because there are so many potential users of information, but it is possible to identify factors which affect the ability of a source to meet the needs of a user, and therefore make it of higher or lower quality within that particular context.

Based upon the above explanation, a complex picture is beginning to emerge:

- different users will define different things as an information source
- different users access and use the Internet for different reasons
- therefore different factors will affect different users' perceptions of the quality of an information source.

This could imply that there are so many possible variables involved in any assessment of quality that the whole process is entirely subjective – in which case there would be no role for a book on the subject. However, it is this understanding of information quality which shapes the content and purpose of this book.

A guide to selection and evaluation

The book is designed to provide guidelines on selection and evaluation without being prescriptive or dictatorial. The next chapter is designed to provide some suggestions of how to approach looking for potentially useful sources. The following chapters on "Assessing the Quality of Any Internet Information Source" (Chapter 3) and "Evaluating Particular Types of Sources" (Chapter 4) provide extensive and detailed guidelines on the wide range of factors which could influence users' perceptions of the quality of the sources they find. However, the book is only intended as a guide, and no one evaluator or Internet user could attempt to address all the criteria which are listed. Readers will need to consider their own needs, or the needs of the user concerned, as well as the nature of the source which is being evaluated. They should then select the appropriate criteria from those which are described.

Furthermore, quality assessment is not a straightforward procedure involving the identification of the presence or absence of different features or facilities. Instead, quality assessment is a complex process involving consideration of a wide range of interrelated issues which are of varying importance depending upon the nature of the source and the needs of the user. For example, while factual accuracy might be important for one user, another might be more interested in the presentation and arrangement of the information. Furthermore, it is sometimes not possible to determine the accuracy of a source, and there are numerous considerations which influence users' perceptions of accuracy, including the knowledge and expertise of the author and the quality of presentation. Due to the complex nature of quality assessment, it is not possible to provide a straightforward list of criteria for use in the evaluation of sources. For this reason, the guidelines provided in this book include detailed explanatory notes on the process of source evaluation and on the relationships between different quality issues. Again, readers will need to consider their needs and the nature of the source concerned, select the appropriate criteria, and apply them as necessary.

References

1. Zakon, R. H., *Hobbe's Internet Timeline* (Version 3.3), 1998, [online]. Available: **http://info.isoc.org/zakon/Internet/History/HIT.html** [1999, April 17].
2. Holderness, M., "Perspective: Why Did the Internet, Brain-Child of Academics and Computer Specialists, Become Such a Cultural Item?," *Times Higher Education Supplement*, April 22, 1994, 17.
3. Elmer-Dewitt, P., "Battle for the Soul of the Internet," *Time International*, **144** (4), 1994, 55.
4. Bower, H., "Internet Sees Growth in Unverified Health Claims," *British Medical Journal*, **313** (7054), 1996, 381.
5. Impicciatore, P., et al., "Reliability of Health Information for the Public on the World Wide Web: Systematic Survey of Advice on Managing Fever in Children at Home," *British Medical Journal*, **314** (7098), 1997, 1875–9.

6. Teskey, F. N., "User Models and World Models for Data, Information and Knowledge," *Information Processing and Management,* **25** (1), 1989, 8.

7. Belkin, N. J., "Towards a definition of information for informatics" in Horsnell, V. (ed.), *Informatics 2: Proceedings of a Conference Held by the ASLIB Co-ordinate Indexing Group, 25–27 March 1974, New College Oxford,* London, Aslib, 1975, 53.

8. British Standards Institution, *Quality Management and Quality Assurance: Vocabulary.* London, British Standards Institution, 1995.

9. Ciolek, T. M. (ed.). *Information Quality: Some Definitions: A Collaborative Gathering of Thoughts and Ideas,* [online]. Available: **http://www.ciolek.com/WWWVLPages/QltyPages/QltyDefinitions.html** [1999, January 11].

2
Using Search Facilities to Maximize Quality Information Retrieval

The first step to finding high-quality sources of information must be to look for them, which is what this chapter is all about. Users often begin by clicking on the "search" button of their WWW browser and using the default engine, only to become frustrated by the huge volume of hits returned and the time taken to sift through the results. However, recent years have seen the development of an increasing number of different facilities, and a vast array are now available which are designed to assist users in searching for information. In particular, certain facilities now concentrate on providing access to high-quality materials.

This chapter provides an overview of the different types of facilities which are available for searching the Internet. For the purposes of comparison, search engines are initially examined before moving on to other types of search facilities:

■ subject catalogs and directories
■ reviewing and rating services
■ subject-based gateway services and virtual libraries.

Examples are provided of each of the different types of search facilities and an explanation is offered of how to use them. Their respective advantages and disadvantages are then considered, particularly in relation to their usefulness when looking for high-quality sources of information. Towards the end of the chapter, tips are provided on where to start searching and when to use which facilities. Finally, a checklist is provided of what to look for in a search tool when seeking high-quality materials.

This chapter is not intended as a general guide to searching the Internet, as this is outside the scope of the book. Instead, the chapter highlights valuable starting places when looking for high-quality materials. Readers who are interested in searching generally should consult one of the many valuable guides to the subject, such as the *Netskills* page on "Searching for information on the

Internet,"[1] the *Search Engine Watch* site,[2] or the materials available from Phil Bradley's home page.[3]

Search engines

Search engines are the most popular means of finding information on the WWW. Search engines, also sometimes called "spiders," "robots," or "crawlers," refer to automatically generated databases of WWW sites and pages. The spider, robot, or crawler constantly visits sites in order to create a database and, because they run automatically and index so many pages, they often contain information not listed by the other tools described later in this chapter. However, they are also the least advantageous when attempting to locate high-quality materials, because they do not discriminate between the quality of the materials which are indexed.

Excite (http://www.excite.com/)

Excite is one example of a search engine. It was launched in late 1995 and quickly became (and remains) a popular tool. *Excite* lists materials in various ways including: "Excite Search," "Channels By Excite," and "Excite News Tracker." "Excite Search" relies on a traditional search engine. The sites in the "channels" area have been evaluated by *Excite* producers who "comb the Web daily looking for the very best that the Web has to offer." Reviews are available for some of the resources listed, and there is also an option to view "Channel highlights" or "Exciting stuff," some of the "most interesting" of the selected sites. "Excite News Tracker" enables users to search listings of speciality news sites. In 1996, *Excite* purchased *Magellan*, a popular reviewing service (discussed under rating and reviewing services), which is run as a separate facility.

Lycos (http://www.lycos.com/)

Lycos has been available since 1994, and is one of the oldest of the major search engines. *Lycos* provides access to resources via two routes: the general search engine, and an additional directory, the "Webguides," guides to resources which have been identified by *Lycos* staff as interesting and potentially useful to Internet users. *Lycos* also runs a rating service called *Top 5%* (discussed under rating and reviewing services).

AltaVista (http://www.altavista.com/)

AltaVista is another very popular search engine, developed by Digital Equipment Corporation in 1995. *AltaVista* not only claims to index 150 million WWW pages, but also allows users to search Usenet newsgroups (although not all of them). As with *Excite* and *Lycos*, in addition to its general engine, *AltaVista* is developing "AltaVista Categories," which provide access to resources categorized into various subject areas. *AltaVista* was the first search engine to offer multilingual searching capabilities, including the ability to search in Chinese, Japanese, and Korean, as well as European languages such as French, German, Italian, Russian, and of course English.

Using a search engine

Suppose that a parent is looking for information on viruses, and wants to know more about the illness which his or her child has. Figure 2.1 displays the search results for "virus" in *Excite*, and as can be seen in the screen shot, 196,099 hits are retrieved. The immense number of results is explained by examining how search engines work. Search engines consist of three major parts: first, the

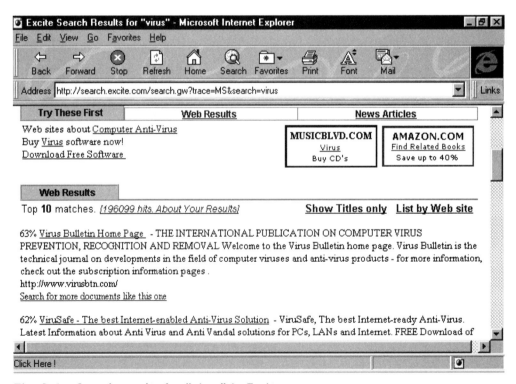

Fig. 2.1 *Search results for "virus" in Excite*

"spider" or "crawler" which visits WWW pages, reads them, and indexes them; second, the database, also sometimes called the catalog or index, which contains a copy of every Web page that the spider finds; and third, the search engine, the program which sifts through the millions of pages in the database to find matches to a user's query. The spider returns to sites regularly (e.g., every week) to look for changes and to update the database, ensuring that its coverage of the WWW is current and extensive. This results in an enormous number of hits for almost any search.

As can be seen in Figure 2.1, *Excite* offers a "try these first" facility, sites which are considered "the cream of the crop – the best sites on the Web that fit your search criteria." The sites have been selected, evaluated, and described by *Excite* staff. However, the suggested sites would be of no interest to a user seeking information about medical viruses as they all relate to viruses of the computer type. The "news articles" are from over 300 of the "Web's best newspapers and magazines" which are searched continually throughout each day. These sound slightly more relevant, as the top five hits (of 114) include "Global distribution of transfusion-transmitted virus" from the *New England Journal of Medicine*, and "More mothers getting AIDS, say doctors" from the *Irish Times*.

Relevance ranking

The main WWW results (Figure 2.1) are listed with those considered most relevant first. The percentage displayed next to each site is the relevance ranking – the higher the figure, the more relevant a site is deemed to be. A page is assumed to be more relevant where the user's search terms appear in the title, where the terms appear near the top of the page, such as in the headline or in the first few paragraphs of text, and where the terms appear frequently in the text. One method which has been used to increase relevance scores in search engine results is "spamming." This involves repeating a word hundreds of times on a page so that the engine assumes it is highly relevant. However, some engines now penalize pages if they detect spamming by ranking them lower than they might otherwise appear in the search results or by excluding them altogether.

Users should not assume that relevance ranking is always successful. As can be seen in Figure 2.1, the first two hits relate to computer viruses. Indeed, not until the user has delved through ten pages of results does anything relating to medical viruses appear. And the result? At number 95 is an electron micrograph of the Ebola virus. Pages which the search engine thinks are relevant, but in fact are not, are frequently listed among the first results; the fact that a word may appear in the title of a page does not necessarily mean that the page is relevant to a particular user.

Narrowing searches down

Excite offers various facilities which can improve the relevance of a set of search results, and other engines offer similar features. As can be seen in Figure 2.1, if a useful site is found, the user can select the option to "search for more documents like this one." In addition, at the top of the search results (not visible in Figure 2.1) various checkboxes are displayed. These are words which are automatically suggested by *Excite* as terms which can be added to a search. The purpose is to help the user identify the particular aspects of a topic which they are interested in. The terms displayed for the search on "virus" are "datafellows," "fellows," "infects," "anti," "infecting," "virusscan," "infected," "infect," "nai," "sodom." Some of these sound possibly useful, but the others are unlikely to be helpful to the parent seeking information on medical viruses. In fact, adding the potentially useful terms (infects, infecting, infected, and infect) provides little benefit in this instance (see Figure 2.2).

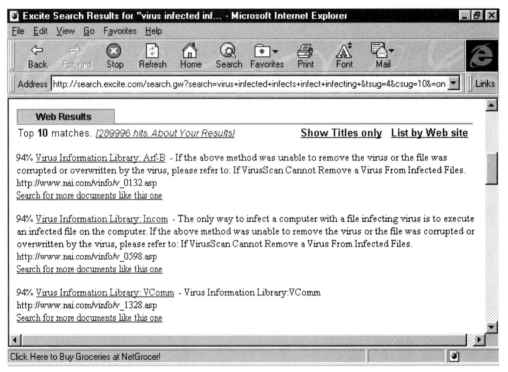

Fig. 2.2 *Search results in Excite for "virus" with "infects," "infecting," "infected," and "infect"*

22

In order to improve the relevance of such a search, the user would obviously need to add the term "medical" to "virus." Having done so, within the first ten hits "Diseases, Disorders, and Related Topics" (**http://www.mic.ki.se/Diseases/index.html**) is retrieved, a site which sounds as if it might be of value to our parent.

Advantages and disadvantages of search engines

Some of the major advantages of search engines have already been mentioned, namely their comprehensive coverage of the WWW and their currency. "Crawlers" or "spiders" search and index the WWW regularly and update the databases with any new sites, as well as with any changes to existing pages. At the time of writing, *AltaVista* claimed to index 150 million WWW pages, and that the database was updated at least once a day. Other plus points include the use of relevance ranking, and different engines offer various features to facilitate retrieval, such as those described for *Excite*. For these reasons, search engines are invaluable where users want extensive coverage of WWW resources and have the time to sift through the vast numbers of sites which are likely to be retrieved.

A further problem is the lack of explanatory information about the materials which are retrieved. Search engines generally rely upon automatically generated summaries which are taken from the first few lines of text in each page, but these are not always a useful indicator of content, as can be seen in Figure 2.2. However, some search engines, such as *AltaVista*, are now beginning to use metadata to generate descriptions. Metadata is information about a WWW page which is written into the HTML of the page but is not displayed by the browser. Authors can include descriptive information about their pages as metadata which is then detected by search engines and displayed in any search results. This generally produces more meaningful descriptions.

A further problem with search engines is that they often include different parts of the same resource within a set of search results. For example, all three pages listed in Figure 2.2 are from the same resource. This repetition occurs because search engines index WWW pages at the individual page level, and therefore different pages from the same site or resource are indexed independently and listed separately in search results. In many circumstances (such as the search results displayed in Figure 2.2) a link to the top-level page of the site or resource would be more helpful.

Another disadvantage is that search engines are restricted to materials which are accessible via the WWW – users interested in locating potentially useful

Usenet newsgroups or discussion lists, for example, must generally use a different search tool.

A lack of discriminatory information

Within the context of this book, the major disadvantage of search engines is that they do not discriminate between materials in terms of their quality. Materials may include subject terms of interest to a user, but they may be irrelevant (as indicated by the example from *Excite*), or the materials retrieved might be outdated, inaccurate, or lacking authority. By adding the term "medical" to the search described above, a potentially relevant site is retrieved. However, retrieval by a search engine does not provide any indication of the quality of the information contained in a resource. Linking to this option might lead the user to outdated or inaccurate material, or to little more than a front page with no detailed information. Search engines work automatically, but there can be no substitute for human judgment when assessing the quality of a source of information. Therefore, when looking for quality sites, users are recommended to consider the other types of search facilities which are discussed later in this chapter, or to use the criteria proposed in the book for assessing the quality of the materials they retrieve.

Further information on search engines

The above overview of search engines and how they work is based on *Excite* as an illustrative example. However, this is only a rough guide. All search engines are slightly different and therefore often return different results for the same search. For more information on the differences between search engines and how they work, as well as further information on which search engines are available and how to use them, *Search Engine Watch* (**http://searchenginewatch. com/**) is an invaluable guide.[2] *Search Engine Watch* is designed for both Webmasters and end users, and provides a comprehensive and frequently updated guide to search engines.

Subject catalogs and directories

Unlike search engines, subject catalogs or directories are created by humans. Sites are submitted by their authors or identified by the site developers and then assigned to an appropriate subject category or categories by the catalog maintainers. Just to confuse matters, many search engines also include a subject catalog element, such as the "Channels By Excite" mentioned earlier, and subject catalogs tend to be both searchable and browsable through a hierarchy of subject headings.

Yahoo! (http://www.yahoo.com/)

Yahoo! is an example of a subject directory. *Yahoo!* was launched in 1994, and claims to be the oldest and largest directory, listing over 750,000 websites divided into more than 25,000 categories. Most of the sites are suggested by users, and each suggestion is examined and evaluated by a member of the *Yahoo!* staff, "whose job it is to decide where the site best belongs." *Yahoo!* is both searchable and browsable.

Galaxy (http://galaxy.einet.net/)

Galaxy was initiated in 1993 and went live in early 1994, and also claims to be the oldest directory. *Galaxy* is similar to *Yahoo!*, being searchable and browsable. Again, authors submit their resources which are then examined by a member of the *Galaxy* staff and allocated to an appropriate subject category or categories.

Using subject catalogs and directories

One reason for using a subject directory might be to look for information for a school child working on a project on the ancient Egyptians. Inputting a search in *Yahoo!* for "ancient Egyptians" results in 56 matches (compared with over 270,000 hits in *Excite*). The results are displayed according to the appropriate subject categories, with a link to the sites concerned and a brief description of each site (see Figure 2.3).

As already mentioned, the majority of sites included in *Yahoo!* are suggested by the site authors themselves. When submitting sites, authors are asked for details about the site, including its name as it will appear in *Yahoo!*, the site address, and a paragraph of up to 25 words describing its contents. Figure 2.3 shows the site name and descriptive information as displayed in the search results. The subject categories are recommended by site authors and then verified by staff involved in developing and maintaining the directory. Within the first few hits, one site, "Ancient Egyptian Information," sounds particularly relevant from the description provided: "Egyptian interactive activities, books, magazines, egyptologists e-mail addresses, archeological digs."

The second approach to accessing information via a subject catalog is to browse the subject categories or headings. From the opening screen of *Yahoo!*,

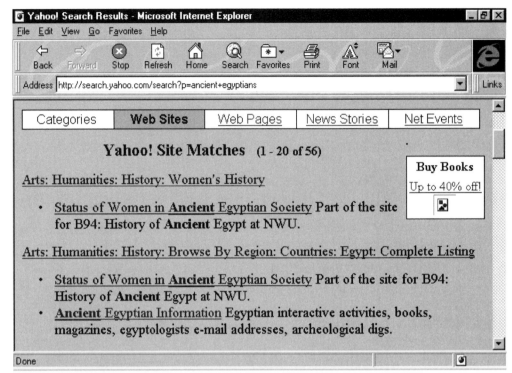

Fig. 2.3 *Search results for "ancient Egyptians" in Yahoo!*

various broad categories are displayed, including arts and humanities, literature, business and economy, computers, education, entertainment, government, health, recreation and sports, regional, science, social science, and society and culture. A user interested in information on the ancient Egyptians would need to select from a range of potentially relevant categories – regional, arts and humanities, social science, society and culture, and perhaps education. Browsing under "regional," followed by "countries," "Egypt," and "society and culture," leads to one site, "Little Horus," described as an "informational site about Egypt, designed for kids." Sounds useful. However, browsing under "arts and humanities," followed by "cultures and groups" and "Egyptian" leads to other potentially relevant resources, as well as a further link to historical materials.

Advantages and disadvantages of subject catalogs and directories

Subject directories and catalogs can provide better results than search engines, as humans are involved in identifying sites and describing their contents. Authors are responsible for describing their own materials and therefore the descriptions are generally more meaningful. Thus, it was relatively easy to determine the potential relevance of materials from the results displayed by *Yahoo!* without having to access the materials themselves. Moreover, different levels of the same resource should not be included in the catalog. Fewer results, less repetition, and more informative descriptions mean that catalogs and directories can be a more efficient way of searching the Internet than search engines.

However, there are drawbacks to human maintenance. The most frequently cited criticism is that subject catalogs and directories are not as comprehensive in their coverage as search engines – *Yahoo!* only covers 750,000 sites in comparison with *AltaVista* which claims to index 150 million WWW pages (although different pages from the same resource might account for a large proportion of this number). Another drawback is that directories are not automatically updated when sites or pages change. For example, *Galaxy* claims to "periodically re-index sites" to "discover (and fix, where possible) bad links" and identify pages which have moved. However, crawlers and robots can update a database daily, ensuring that it is always current.

A further disadvantage of particular interest here is that subject catalogs and directories do not discriminate between sites in terms of their quality. Those involved in developing and maintaining the tools are concerned with the subject relevance of materials and not necessarily with their quality – this contrasts with virtual libraries and subject-based gateway services in particular, where humans are involved in identifying potentially relevant resources and also in evaluating their quality (see below).

Further information on subject catalogs and directories

Yahoo! is frequently described alongside search engines, although it is fundamentally different, and the sources of further information already mentioned include catalogs and directories.[1-3] However, less information is available about the directory components of search engines. In order to find out about these, try reading through the help pages for the engines themselves, where explanatory material is usually offered about the different search options which are available. For example, a link to the help pages is available at the end of the opening screen of *Excite*, and includes details about *Excite's* "channels" (**http://www.excite.com/Info/**).

Rating and reviewing services

During the mid-1990s, there was a trend towards providing more effective access to Internet materials through various forms of site ratings and reviews. Many of these services have been developed, of varying value and usefulness, and some have already been and gone. However, there are a few notable examples that remain. These facilities tend to include materials of popular appeal and cover a wide range of subject areas.

Encyclopaedia Britannica's Internet Guide (http://www.ebig.com/)

The *Encyclopaedia Britannica's Internet Guide*, or *eBlast*, is a fairly new guide which covers more than 125,000 WWW sites and is produced by the well-known encyclopaedia publisher, Encyclopaedia Britannica. Britannica editors "search the Web to identify the highest-quality Web resources, which are then clearly and concisely described, rated according to consistent standards, and indexed for superior retrieval."

Lycos Top 5% (http://point.lycos.com/)

Some search engines offer an associated directory of rated and reviewed resources in addition to the engine itself and its directory component. *Lycos* was among the earliest of the Internet search engines, and in the mid-1990s it purchased one of the earliest rating services, *Point*. *Point* was launched in 1995 and aimed to list what its editors considered to be the top 5% of all WWW sites. When *Lycos* acquired the service it maintained the ethos but changed the name.

Magellan Internet Guide (http://www.mckinley.com/magellan/)

As mentioned earlier, in 1996 *Excite* purchased the *Magellan Internet Guide*, a rating service which is run independently from the search engine. Sites are reviewed by "Magellan's experts," and the service boasts over 60,000 reviews. A search in *Magellan* results in a brief description of resources, ranked according to their relevance, with a star rating designed to indicate quality.

Using rating and reviewing services

Suppose that a postgraduate student studying for her M.S. is looking for further information on international relations. The name "Britannica" suggests an authoritative and useful guide to Internet resources. The opening screen of *eBlast* displays a query input box, with an option to include results from a search engine (*AltaVista*), and a number of browsable subject headings (e.g., arts and literature, business, computers, entertainment and leisure, health and medicine, history, news and current events, philosophy and religion, and science and technology).

Figure 2.4 displays some of the matches to a search for "international relations" in *eBlast*. As can be seen, the results include a brief description about each resource and a star rating – sites are awarded five stars for "best of the Web," four for "superior," three for "excellent," two for "recommended," one for "noteworthy," and no stars for "unrated." Further information is also provided about the sites under "site info," and the appropriate subject categories are listed. The second resource displayed could be of value to an M.S. student, as it is described as a "clearinghouse for resources in the field of security and defense studies, peace and conflict research, and international relations," and has been awarded four stars.

eBlast has similar access facilities to the general subject catalogs. However, authors can only recommend sites for inclusion in *eBlast*. When sites have been recommended, they are examined and evaluated by *eBlast* staff to determine whether they are appropriate for inclusion in the service. Sites are judged according to their accuracy, completeness, utility, the credentials and authority of the publisher, frequency of revision, quality and effectiveness of presentation,

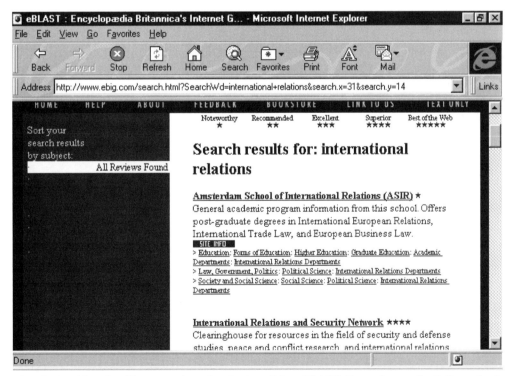

Fig. 2.4 *Hits for "international relations" in eBLAST, Encyclopaedia Britannica's Internet Guide*

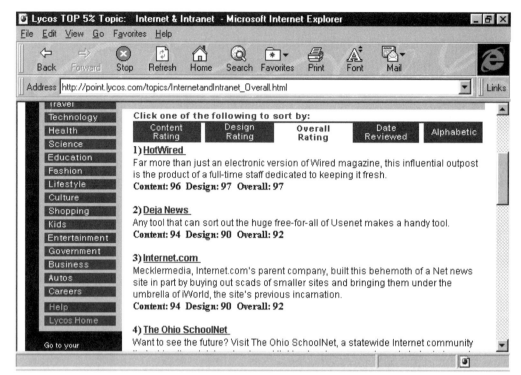

Fig. 2.5 *Browsing "technology" and "Internet and Intranet" in Lycos Top 5%.*
© 1998 Lycos, Inc. Lycos ® is a registered trademark of Carnegie Mellon
University. All rights reserved.

elegance of design, and the quality of the graphics. They are then awarded a star rating and assigned to appropriate subject categories.

Rather than using a star rating scheme, the *Lycos Top 5%* service rates sites numerically. Browsing the *Lycos Top 5%* service for "technology," followed by "Internet and Intranet" results in the screen displayed in Figure 2.5. Each site is awarded three scores from zero to 100 for its content, design, and overall usefulness. The meaning of the scores is defined as follows:

> If scores were classic rock bands, this is what they'd sound like.
>
> 100–90: The Beatles, Rolling Stones, Bob Dylan . . . not only good but important and influential. Sites that signal a leading trend on the Internet.
>
> 89–80: The Who, Joni Mitchell, Beach Boys . . . strong but occasionally uneven work. Niche sites with strong potential and areas of importance.
>
> 79–70: Led Zeppelin, Elton John, The Doors . . . broad appeal but sometimes lacking ideas. Sites that may be useful but not necessarily inspired or compelling.

69–60: James Taylor, John Denver, Billy Joel . . . relatively ordinary. Standard-issue sites that lack originality.

59–50: Garth Brooks, Celine Dion, Sheryl Crow . . . a typical Grammy evening. Sites that barely make the Lycos TOP 5% cut.

49–01: Unusually low quality, for sites that have zero content and a dramatic lack of visual appeal. Obviously, scoring more than once in this range excludes membership in the TOP 5% directory.

As shown in Figure 2.5, there is a brief descriptive review of each site plus the numerical scores. The results can be ranked according to the scores for the three different rating categories, and it is also possible to access a full review for each site (Figure 2.6).

The *Lycos Top 5%* service also awards badges to those sites included in the *Top 5%*. These badges can be displayed by the site concerned as an indicator of quality. Various other services have adopted this approach, including *Magellan*, and it is sometimes possible to see a collection of such badges at the end of a page or by following a link which reads something like "click here to see our awards. . . ." One such example is the "Philosophy around the Web" guide (**http://users.ox.ac.uk/%7Eworc0337/phil_index.html**) which includes a link

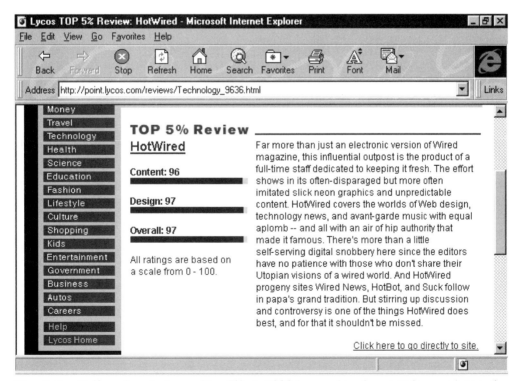

Fig. 2.6 *Full review in Lycos Top 5%. © 1998 Lycos, Inc. Lycos ® is a registered trademark of Carnegie Mellon University. All rights reserved.*

("Reviews and Awards") to some of the badges which the site has been awarded (**http://users.ox.ac.uk/~worc0337/reviews.html**).

Advantages and disadvantages of rating and reviewing services

In 1997, *Internet World* voted *Lycos Top 5%* "best" of a range of reviewing services and argued that the service saves the user time in "pursuit of quality information."[4] Rating and reviewing services use star ratings and numerical scores to indicate the quality of a site at a glance. For example, it is easy to identify the most highly rated sites from the results in *eBlast* or *Lycos Top 5%* by glancing at the number of stars or scores allocated. Consequently, this can reduce significantly the time taken to sift through search results. Likewise, if a user is browsing the WWW and finds a site with various badges and awards, such as those produced by *Lycos Top 5%* or *Magellan*, he or she can be confident that a third party has evaluated the site and considered it worth recommending to others.

One advantage these services share with subject catalogs is that the descriptions or reviews are created manually and therefore usually offer a more meaningful insight into the content of the resources than is the case with search engines. The reviews provided by these services are more detailed than the descriptions provided in subject catalogs – for example, compare the level of detail and meaningfulness of the descriptions in Figure 2.2 (taken from a search engine) with Figure 2.3 (a subject catalog), and with Figure 2.6 (a full review from *Lycos Top 5%*).

However, there are many drawbacks and problems with rating and reviewing services. Owing to the level of human input required in selecting, evaluating, and describing resources, these services tend to be much smaller and less comprehensive than search engines. Many of the services form part of a general search engine, and in this case it is possible to automatically expand a search using the engine if no sites are retrieved in the rating service. However, the rating services do not appear as the default option when a query is made to a search engine, and as a rule users must consciously choose to see the reviews. Moreover, with the exception of *eBLAST* and *Lycos Top 5%*, the sites generally lack information about how they have selected and evaluated the resources.

A true indication of site quality?

In the context of this book, the main controversy in relation to these services is whether they truly indicate the quality of information sources. Authors within the library profession have compared a range of different services in order to examine the approaches used for evaluating and describing resources, and also to consider their effectiveness in guiding users towards quality materials.[5-8] The use of badges to indicate site quality has also been examined.[9] The general conclusion is that rating and reviewing services offer little indication of site quality. Indeed, one person argues that the "criteria for inclusion and the rating scale are highly impressionistic, and descriptive notes on each site are minimalist."[5] Furthermore, "the impressionistic 'cool' counts for a great deal" and the "ratings are useless except to those who hold the same subjective preconceptions."[5] The use of badges "vary so widely in their implementation and interpretation, it remains questionable whether they can succeed in guiding the user to the selection of high-quality resources "at a glance'."[9]

One of the major problems of rating and reviewing services is that they have no clearly defined audience, but appear to be designed for popular appeal, i.e. to any Internet user. In the previous chapter, quality was defined in terms of the extent to which an information source meets the needs of the user. The users of the Internet are vast in number, and therefore, by adopting an all-embracing approach, these services are perhaps less likely to meet the quality aspirations of particular individuals. Alternatively, "because any consideration of quality is highly subjective, services with a subject and audience focus are more likely to serve the needs of their users."[10]

Readers are therefore recommended to consider using one of the more formal services discussed below under "virtual libraries and subject-based gateway services" when looking for high-quality materials, but to note that rating and reviewing services do offer many advantages over search engines and subject directories. The resources included in rating and reviewing services have at least been through a process of selection and evaluation. However, when using these services, readers should be aware of their limitations (that they are designed for popular appeal and may not be suitable for all audiences), and after retrieving any materials via these services, users are recommended to apply the criteria discussed in Chapters 3 and 4.

Further information on rating and reviewing services

The various references which have been mentioned in the above section provide further information on different rating and reviewing services.[5-10] In particular, readers are recommended to examine Cooke, A. et al.,[7] which compares the facilities offered by various popular services with other search tools. In addition, the article by McNab, A. et al.[9] considers the value and usefulness of different badges which WWW sites can display as a sign of quality.

Subject-based gateway services and virtual libraries

The final category of search facilities are those services which have been designed by librarians and/or subject experts with the explicit aim of providing access to high quality sources of information. Some of these are described as "virtual libraries," while others are described as "subject-based gateway services."

The Argus Clearinghouse (http:// www.clearinghouse.net/)

The *Argus Clearinghouse* is an evaluative guide to evaluative guides. Staff at the *Clearinghouse* evaluate, categorize, and describe "value-added topical guides which identify, describe, and evaluate Internet-based information resources." The *Clearinghouse* covers guides to Internet resources in a wide range of subject areas, including the arts and humanities, business, government and law, health and medicine, recreation, the sciences, and the social sciences. The *Clearinghouse* is the most obvious starting place for users embarking on a quest for quality materials, because it provides a gateway to other services which provide access to high-quality resources. The service is therefore discussed further under "where to start" (towards the end of the chapter).

BUBL Link (http://bubl.ac.uk/link/)

BUBL, the *Bulletin Board for Libraries*, is a centrally funded national information service for the higher education community in the UK. *BUBL Link*, originally the *BUBL Subject Tree*, was established in 1993 by the UK Office for Library Networking. Now based at the University of Strathclyde, *BUBL Link* is a searchable and browsable catalog of selected Internet resources. A team of library and information professionals is involved in the selection and evaluation of resources, which are then described and categorized. *BUBL* has recently introduced *BUBL 5:15*. The aim of this service is to help users to find networked materials about a range of subjects; it provides at least five relevant resources on each subject, but usually no more than fifteen.

CyberStacks (http://www.public.iastate.edu/~CYBERSTACKS/)

CyberStacks was formally established in November 1995 at Iowa State University as a collection of "significant" Internet resources. Materials are selected and evaluated according to traditional guidelines used within librarianship, and then categorized using the Library of Congress classification scheme. Users can browse through the subject headings to identify potentially relevant resources, and for each resource a description is provided. At present, *CyberStacks* is a prototype demonstration service and is limited to significant resources of a research or scholarly nature in selected fields (geography, anthropology, recreation, social sciences, science, medicine, agriculture, and technology), but there are plans for its continued development.

The eLib subject-based information gateways (http://ukoln.ac.uk/services/elib/projects/)

In 1993, an investigation was undertaken in the UK into how to deal with pressures on library resources caused by the rapid expansion of student numbers and the worldwide explosion in academic knowledge and information. This led to the *Electronic Libraries Programme, eLib* (**http://ukoln.ac.uk/services/elib/**), a centrally funded national program of research in the UK into the role and development of the "electronic library." There are various themes within *eLib*, one of which is "access to networked resources." It is within this area that the following subject-based information gateways have been developed:

- *ADAM* (**http://www.adam.ac.uk/**), the *Art, Design, Architecture, and Media Information Gateway*
- *Biz/ed* (**http://www.bized.ac.uk/**), the *Business and Economics Gateway*
- *EEVL* (**http://www.eevl.ac.uk/**), the *Edinburgh Engineering Virtual Library*
- *OMNI* (**http://omni.ac.uk/**), *Organizing Medical Networked Information*
- *RUDI* (**http://rudi.herts.ac.uk/**), *Resources for Urban Design Information*
- *SOSIG* (**http://sosig.ac.uk/**), the *Social Science Information Gateway*.

Each of the gateways is slightly different. However, most provide access to a searchable and browsable database of Internet resource descriptions within their particular subject area. Resources are selected and evaluated by library professionals and/or subject experts. Records are then manually created to provide meaningful and informative descriptions, and resources are also described using traditional cataloging and classification methods to enable more effective retrieval. These services are generally aimed at the UK higher education community, although they do have a much wider appeal, and they have each been developed by a different consortium of partners, usually within the academic arena.

Infomine: scholarly Internet resource collections (http://lib-www.ucr.edu/)

Infomine began in January 1994 as a service provided by the library of the University of California, Riverside. The service is now developed collaboratively by librarians at all nine University of California campuses and Stanford University, and is intended for use by faculty, students, and research staff. It has been developed as "a showcase, virtual library, and reference tool containing highly useful Internet/Web resources." *Infomine* currently provides access to over 14,000 "academically valuable resources" within a range of areas (biological, agricultural and medical sciences, government information, instructional resources, physical sciences, engineering, computing, maths, regional and general interest, social sciences, humanities, and visual and performing arts). Within each area, a searchable and browsable database of resource descriptions is available.

The Internet Public Library (http://www.ipl.org/)

The *Internet Public Library* is a guide to the types of resources which might be found in a public library, including reference materials, exhibitions, newspapers and magazines, full-text materials, and sources for "teen" and "youth" audiences. The materials are identified, evaluated, cataloged, and described. The idea for the service arose from a seminar held in the School of Information and Library Studies at the University of Michigan in 1995, and it was launched in March 1995. It is now well established, with three full-time members of library staff, and receives external funding from the W. K. Kellogg Foundation as well as gifts from "Friends of the Library."

Librarians' Index to the Internet (http://sunsite.berkeley.edu/InternetIndex/index.html)

The *Librarians' Index to the Internet* is a directory of more than 3,800 Internet resource descriptions. The resources have all been selected and evaluated by 67 librarians from around California "for their usefulness to the public library user's information needs." The service was started in 1990 as a reference librarian's Gopher bookmark file, but later moved to Berkeley Public Library and became the "Berkeley Public Library Index to the Internet." In March 1997, the service became the *Librarians' Index to the Internet*. The *Index* is both browsable and searchable, and each resource is categorized under different subject headings, with a description of its content. The resource description is detailed and informative, offering insight into the content of the resource and its potential value.

The SCOUT Report (http://wwwscout.cs.wisc.edu/scout/)

The *SCOUT Report*, first started in 1995, is different from the other services described above as it is an e-mail service which "provides a fast, convenient way to stay informed of valuable resources on the Internet." The service is produced by library professionals and subject experts who identify, evaluate, and describe valuable resources. A newsletter containing the descriptions is e-mailed every Friday to thousands of subscribers. The newsletter is also published on the WWW, and it is possible to browse previous newsletters by subject area (arts and humanities, business, law, medicine and health, sciences, social sciences, etc.), and according to the newsletter dates. The project is located at the Department of Computer Sciences at the University of Wisconsin-Madison, and is funded by a grant from the National Science Foundation.

Using subject-based gateway services and virtual libraries

SOSIG, the *Social Sciences Information Gateway*, is one of the gateway services developed under *eLib*. The service is aimed at social scientists in higher education and research, and covers a wide range of subjects including education, environmental issues, feminism, geography, law, philosophy, politics, psychology, and sociology. *SOSIG* offers various access facilities, including browsing different subject headings or searching the database. Browsing for "women" followed by "Women's suffrage" leads to nine results, the first of which is displayed in Figure 2.7.

Resource selection, evaluation, and description

As with the other services included in this section, *SOSIG* provides access to the descriptions of high-quality resources only. Every resource has been selected and evaluated using explicit criteria (**http://sosig.ac.uk/desire/ecrit.html**) which relate not only to the presentation of information but also to its subject coverage, currency, accuracy, and reliability. Following evaluation, high-quality sources are described by a librarian or subject specialist, and the descriptions are included in the database. Different subject specialists are responsible for the collection management and maintenance of particular areas of the service, as well as monitoring whether sites are out-of-date or no longer available. As

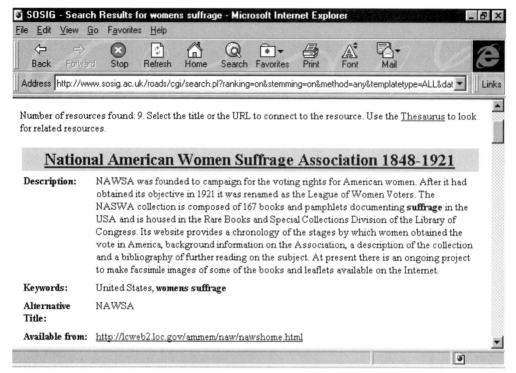

Fig. 2.7 *Resource description in SOSIG*

shown in Figure 2.7, *SOSIG* provides a detailed description of each resource, which indicates coverage, value, and usefulness to the user.

Figure 2.8 displays a record retrieved from the *Librarians' Index to the Internet*. This service is run in much the same way as *SOSIG*, but the materials which it covers are of interest to public library users.

Cataloging and classification

In addition to the descriptions provided by these services, many of them also use traditional methods of cataloging and classification to describe the resources and enable them to be retrieved easily. For example, in *SOSIG*, librarians create a catalog record for each resource. The record is similar to any record in a normal library system and contains information such as the title, description, subject keywords, and site address. The records are added to the *SOSIG* database, and when a user searches the database, they are searching the information held in the catalog rather than the resources themselves. This ensures "higher precision . . . as librarians have ensured that the descriptions and keywords in the catalog are carefully chosen to help users find relevant information."

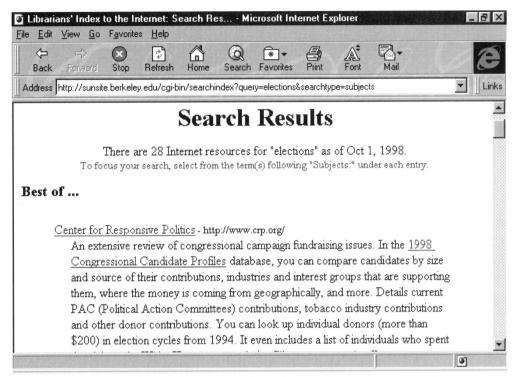

Fig. 2.8 *Resource description in the Librarians' Index to the Internet*

Sources are also browsable through the use of a classification scheme. Again using the example of *SOSIG*, a traditional scheme (the Universal Decimal Classification scheme or UDC) is used to classify resources based upon the subject area to which they relate. The scheme used is a standard classification scheme which is used in libraries throughout the world to organize materials on library shelves. Once the resources have been appropriately classified, they are then automatically arranged in *SOSIG* according to these classifications into browsable lists of subject headings.

Advantages and disadvantages of subject-based gateway services and virtual libraries

The main advantage of subject-based gateway services and virtual libraries is that they provide access to detailed descriptions of high-quality resources. They are developed and maintained by information professionals and/or subject experts, and the user can access these services assured in the knowledge that an individual working in the field has already identified and evaluated relevant high-quality resources. This relieves the user of much of the work in filtering potentially useful sources from the vast quantities of dross available via the Internet. As indicated by the example from *SOSIG*, the descriptions are intended to provide an accurate, concise, and meaningful indication of the value and usefulness of the materials, saving the user from linking to irrelevant, outdated, or inaccurate sites.

Narrow audience focus

One of the problems mentioned in relation to reviewing and rating services was their undefined audience – such services are aimed at any Internet user, and therefore it is difficult to imagine how the resources which are included in them can relate to a particular user's quality needs. The services included in this section have identified a specific audience. For example, *OMNI* (one of the *eLib* gateways) is aimed at health care and medical users in higher education or research. As already discussed, quality is a subjective issue, and one individual's source of quality information is likely to be another individual's dross. Therefore, the more clearly and narrowly defined the audience focus of a service, the easier it is for users to decide whether the material it covers is likely to match their own needs.

Explicit evaluation criteria

Another advantage is that the criteria used by these services for evaluation are explicit: there is often a document describing the criteria or a collection development policy – see for example the *OMNI Guidelines for Resource Evaluation* (**http://omni.ac.uk/agec/evalguid.html**). These criteria are designed to assess a range of factors which affect the quality of an information source, including accuracy, reliability, currency, and coverage. Consequently, users can examine the evaluation criteria in order to determine whether they match the aspects of quality assessment they are interested in.

Further advantages

A further advantage of subject-based gateway services and virtual libraries is that they cover the full range of Internet materials. Search engines, subject catalogs, and rating services tend to be restricted to WWW-based materials. In order to search, for example, discussion lists or FTP archives, a separate search facility is generally required. However, the services in this section do not discriminate between materials according to their format, and it is therefore possible to search all types of materials via one tool. Furthermore, there is less repetition in the search results, because resources are evaluated and described at the resource level as opposed to the individual page level used by search engines. Another advantage is the use of traditional cataloging and classification techniques which, as discussed earlier, aims to ensure accurate subject description and to facilitate the retrieval of resources.

Limitations

However, these services do have disadvantages, similar to those already mentioned in relation to subject catalogs and rating and reviewing services. The high level of human input involved in developing and maintaining these services means that they cover a relatively small number of materials, and they cannot be updated as frequently as search engines. In addition, the narrow audience and subject focus means that a service such as *OMNI* which covers resources relating to health care and medicine for higher education and research will be of little interest to a lay person who does not have a high level of knowledge and understanding in the field.

Further information on subject-based gateway services and virtual libraries

Only a small number of subject-based gateway services and virtual libraries have been discussed here. As mentioned, an invaluable place to find out about the vast number of other evaluative guides which are available is the *Argus Clearinghouse* (discussed in detail under "where to start"). In addition, many of the references mentioned in relation to rating and reviewing services also consider subject-based gateway services and virtual.[5–10] Some of the guides to Internet searching generally also consider virtual libraries,[1,3] and Anna Brümmer has created a list of subject-based information gateways with factual details about each service.[11]

Speciality search tools

The options for searching the Internet are far more extensive than those which have been described here, and it is almost impossible to categorize all of the different facilities. There are specialist services for searching news information and for searching for people or e-mail addresses, as well as tools for searching specific types of resources (e.g., software, images, reference materials, Usenet newsgroups, and discussion lists). It is also possible to access some of the facilities which have already been mentioned via a local mirror site, as well as to search specialist tools for UK or other regional-based information sources. As mentioned earlier, this chapter is not intended as a general guide to searching the

Internet, as this is outside the scope of the book, and it would be impossible to do justice to all the other search facilities which are currently available. Some references have already been provided for further information on searching generally,[1-3] and one particularly useful resource on speciality search facilities is the *Netskills* page on "Further searching for information on the Internet."[12]

Meta-search engines

Meta-search engines, also sometimes called meta-crawlers or multisearch engines, enable users to search several search tools at once rather than searching a single database. The results are then presented together, generally in one page.

iSleuth.com (http://www.isleuth.com/)

iSleuth.com, or "*The Sleuth*," is an example of a multisearch engine. *The Sleuth* claims to cover over 3,000 searchable databases, including a range of specialist search tools (e.g., rating and reviewing services and news services), as well as general search engines. The users select the databases they wish to search from the query input screen (Figure 2.9) and they then type in their search terms.

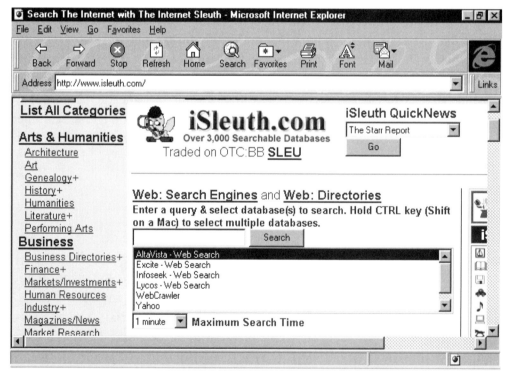

Fig. 2.9 *Search input screen for The Sleuth*

The results are displayed under headings for each of the different databases which have been selected – Figure 2.10 displays the results for "virus" listed for the *WebCrawler* search engine (**http://webcrawler.com/**). The results are displayed in the same format in which they would appear when using each search engine independently, and therefore, when scrolling through the results, users are presented with different results in different formats. *The Sleuth* does not remove duplicates, and so the same sites may be listed repeatedly under the different search tools.

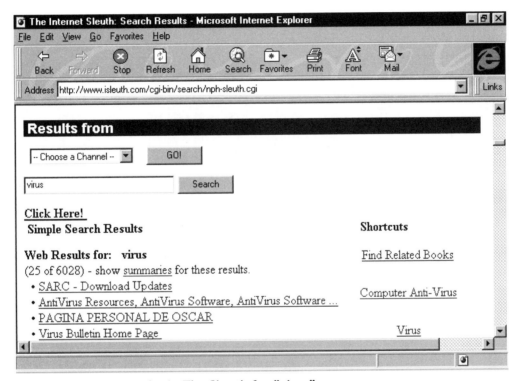

Fig. 2.10 *Search results in The Sleuth for "virus"*

SavvySearch (http://www.savvysearch.com)

SavvySearch works in a similar way to *The Sleuth* as it is designed to query 19 search engines simultaneously. Users input their search and specify the number of results desired from each engine. When a query has been submitted, the 19 search engines are ranked according to various factors, including the estimated Internet traffic, the anticipated response time of remote search engines, and the load on the computer. As with *The Sleuth*, the results are then displayed in groupings according to the different search engines.

Advantages and disadvantages of meta-search engines

There are numerous meta-search engines available, and each works in a slightly different way, offering slightly different advantages and disadvantages. The two sites described above allow users to conduct a simultaneous search on multiple databases, thus ensuring more comprehensive coverage of the WWW than would otherwise be possible. As a result, these tools are invaluable where comprehensiveness is a major aim. Another meta-search engine, *Metasearch* (**http://www.metasearch.com/**), works by linking users to a range of different engines which they then search as normal. Advantages of this approach include easy access to a range of different search tools without needing to type in the site addresses, and notifying users of alternative tools which they might not have otherwise considered.

However, the main drawback to meta-search engines must be the volume of resources which are retrieved in response to a query. The results displayed in Figure 2.10 list 25 hits from a possible 6,028 from one search engine only. The same search results in 1,763,030 matches in *AltaVista* and 1,050,497 matches in *Infoseek* (**http://www.infoseek.com/**). Indeed, the disadvantages already described in relation to search engines will only be multiplied by concurrently searching a number of them, namely:

- the huge number of hits for any one search
- the lack of explanatory information about the material which is retrieved
- the inclusion of links to different pages within the same resource
- the time taken to sift through search results
- a restriction to WWW-based materials
- a lack of discrimination between materials in terms of their quality.

Further information on meta-search engines

Phil Bradley has conducted a useful comparison of seven meta-search engines, and this includes a more detailed explanation of how they work, the number of search tools each covers, and the different facilities which are available for each.[13] In addition, *Search Engine Watch* provides an extensive list of the various tools which are available with a brief description of each.[14]

Where to start

This chapter has examined a range of facilities for searching the Internet, from the most heavily used search engines which aim for comprehensive coverage of the WWW, through subject directories and rating and reviewing services, to highly selective services, and finally speciality search tools and meta-search engines. So, where should readers start? The first task when looking for quality is to attempt to locate a site or service which provides access to high-quality materials within the subject area of interest. A limited number of such services have been discussed under "subject-based gateway services and virtual libraries," but as mentioned, an invaluable guide, and probably the best starting place from which to reach the vast number of guides which are available, is the *Argus Clearinghouse*.

Using the Argus Clearinghouse

As mentioned earlier, the *Argus Clearinghouse* is an evaluative guide to evaluative guides; it covers "value-added topical guides which identify, describe, and evaluate Internet-based information resources."

The *Clearinghouse* is both searchable and browsable. Browsing under the heading "arts and humanities," followed by "history," and lastly "Vietnam War" leads to the results displayed in Figure 2.11. The titles of three guides are displayed, with subject headings indicating their coverage, and an overall rating of between one and five ticks which is designed to indicate their quality. Of the

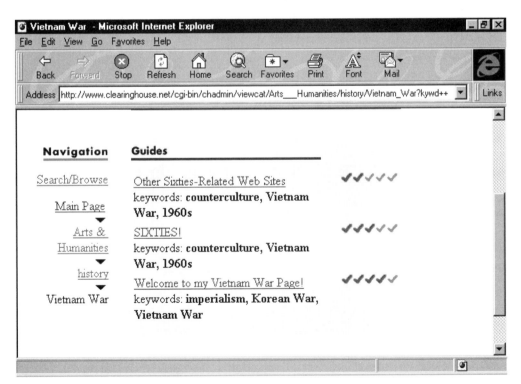

Fig. 2.11 *Guides for "Vietnam War" included in the Argus Clearinghouse*

three guides displayed, "Welcome to my Vietnam War Page!" should be the most valuable as it has four out of five ticks. This might surprise some readers as the title suggests a personal home page which perhaps links to a few sites of interest. However, the guides in the *Clearinghouse* are evaluated and reviewed by "dedicated individuals who either have or are studying for Master's Degrees in Information and Library Science," and only 5 to 10 percent of the guides submitted to the *Clearinghouse* are included – so the ratings should be reasonably reliable.

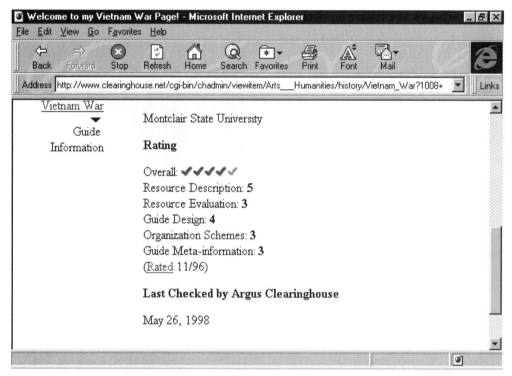

Fig. 2.12 *Details of "Welcome to my Vietnam War Page!" in the Argus Clearinghouse*

Clicking on the link to "Welcome to my Vietnam War Page!" leads to the review displayed in Figure 2.12. Guides are submitted to the *Clearinghouse* by their authors and evaluated by *Clearinghouse* staff according to an explicit rating system. The criteria relate to the level of resource description, the level of resource evaluation, the guide design, the organizational schemes used in the guide, and the use of metadata. As can be seen in Figure 2.12, guides receive between one and five "ticks" for each criteria, and an overall average score is awarded. Other information (not all displayed in Figure 2.12) includes details of the organization or individual responsible for the guide, subject descriptors, the date the *Clearinghouse* last checked the site, and a link to the site itself.

Nothing turns up?

Two problems might arise at this stage:

- users cannot find a guide which covers the subject area that they are interested in
- users find a guide covering the appropriate area, but there is nothing of interest in it.

The type of services included in the *Clearinghouse*, and discussed under "subject-based gateway services and virtual libraries," generally aim for coverage of high-quality materials only. However, owing to the level of human input required in identifying, evaluating, and describing materials, they often cover only a relatively small number of resources and they are often of interest to only a limited number of users. Consequently, there may not be a selective search tool available which covers the appropriate subject area, and the available services may not contain any relevant materials.

Broadening a search

If a guide is not available, or nothing turns up in the search results, readers should first consider modifying the search terms they are using. It may be possible to find a relevant guide by using a much broader search term. For example, a user looking for information on Saigon during the Vietnam War is unlikely to find a specific guide on "Saigon." However, using the broader terms "Vietnam" or "history" might lead to guides which contain appropriate information. After finding an apparently relevant guide, the search terms can also be broadened. For example, had "international relations" proved too narrow when searching the *Britannica Internet Guide* (Figure 2.4), the search might have been broadened to "political science."

If there are still no results in a relevant guide, users should then move through the types of search facilities which have been described in this chapter in the following order:

1. rating and reviewing services
2. general subject catalogs and directories
3. search engines
4. meta-search engines.

If a highly selective guide is not available or contains no relevant materials, the rating and reviewing services are less focused, but the use of numerical scores or

47

star ratings can be useful in indicating recommended sites at a glance when sifting through the search results. General subject directories or catalogs should be the next option. These tend to be larger again but less selective in terms of site quality. However, the descriptions generally offer a meaningful indication of the content of the resources. If still nothing useful is found, now might be the time to try a search engine. These offer the most comprehensive coverage of the WWW, but are the least discriminating and the least descriptive about the sites they cover. Therefore, users will need to expend more time and effort in filtering through the search results. Finally, if still nothing turns up, a meta-search engine is the final option. A tool such as *The Sleuth* (discussed earlier) claims to cover over 3,000 databases, including directories and some rating and reviewing sites, as well as various search engines. If still nothing is found after using a meta-search engine, now might be the time to suspect there is nothing suitable on the Internet!

Some tools offer the option to broaden a search automatically. For example, following a search in *Yahoo!*, users can search the engine, *Inktomi* (**http://www.inktomi.com/**). Figure 2.3 displays the search results in *Yahoo!* for "ancient Egyptians." As can be seen in the screen shot, the "Web Sites" option is highlighted – selecting the "Web pages" option will automatically search

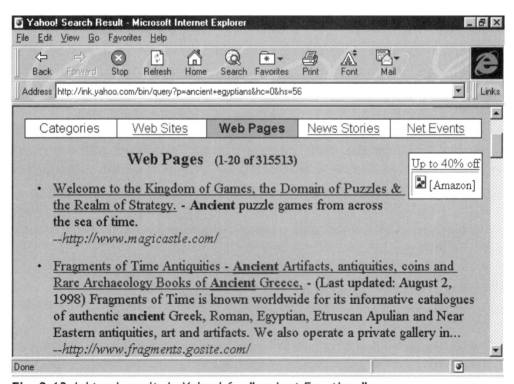

Fig. 2.13 *Inktomi results in Yahoo! for "ancient Egyptians"*

Inktomi. The results are displayed in Figure 2.13 – over 30,000 results are retrieved, compared with 56 by searching *Yahoo!*. Similarly, the *Britannica Internet Guide* offers the option of searching *eBLAST* only or also *AltaVista*.

Summary of the advantages and disadvantages of different types of search tools

Figure 2.14 summarizes the main advantages and disadvantages of different search facilities. As a general rule, the greater the number of resources covered by a search tool, the less selective the guide is in terms of the quality of the materials included in it, and the less descriptive information there is likely to be.

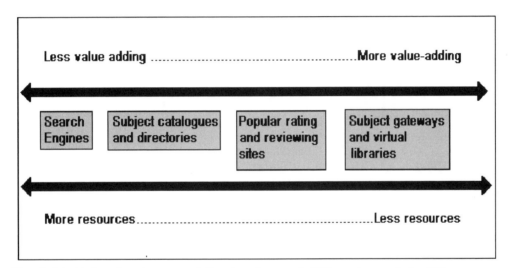

Fig. 2.14 *Main advantages and disadvantages of different search facilities*

CHECKLIST

What to look for in a search tool

This chapter has provided various suggestions on which search tools to use and when to use them, as well as outlining the advantages and disadvantages of different types of search facilities. To summarize, when choosing a search tool in order to look for high-quality information sources, the main questions to consider are:

☑ What subject areas does the search tool cover?

☑ Who are the intended users of the tool?

☑ Are resources selected and evaluated for inclusion in the database?

☑ Are resources awarded a rating according to their perceived quality?

☑ Are explicit evaluation criteria available which explain how resources are evaluated and on what basis?

☑ Are descriptions provided about each resource, and do the resource descriptions provide sufficient information to enable you to assess their relevance?

☑ Are the resource descriptions evaluative? Do they indicate the likely value and usefulness of the materials?

☑ How frequently are materials revisited to ensure their continuing value and usefulness?

☑ What is the knowledge and expertise of those involved in selecting, evaluating, and describing materials?

☑ What types of materials does the search tool cover? Does it only include information available via the WWW, or are other materials also covered?

It is also worth considering:

☑ What search options are available?

☑ Are there facilities to narrow and broaden searches?

☑ Is it possible to browse by subject categories, and are the subject headings or categories meaningful?

☑ Are the different options effective, easy to use, and useful?

☑ Is any help information available which provides guidelines on using the tool? Is the help information clear and understandable? Is it useful?

References

1. *Searching for Information on the Internet,* [online], 1998. Available: http://www.netskills.ac.uk/support/searching/search1.html [1999, January 11].

2. Sullivan, D., *Search Engine Watch*, [online], 1998. Available: http://searchenginewatch.com/ [1999, January 11].

3. Bradley, P., *Welcome to Phil's Home Page*, [online], 1998. Available: http://www.philb.com/ [1999, January 11].

4. Venditto, G., "Sites that Rate the Web: Critic's Choice," *Internet World*, 8 (1), 1997, 84.

5. Rettig, J., "Beyond 'Cool': Analog Models for Reviewing Digital Resources," *Online* [online], September, 1996. Available: http://www.onlineinc.com/onlinemag/SeptOL/rettig9.html [1999, January 11].

6. Tillman, H. N., *Evaluating Quality on the Net*, [online], 1997. Available: http://www.tiac.net/users/hope/findqual.html [1999, January 11].

7. Cooke, A. et al., "The Good, the Bad and the Ugly: Internet Review Sites," in Raitt, D. I. and Jeapes, B. (eds.), *Proceedings of the 20th International Online Information Meeting*, Oxford, Learned Information, 20, 1996, 33–40.

8. Collins, B. R., "Beyond Cruising: Reviewing," *Library Journal*, 121 (3), 1996, 124.

9. McNab, A. et al., "Never Mind the Quality, Check the Badge-Width," *Ariadne*, [online] 9, 1997, 6–7. Available: http://www.ariadne.ac.uk/Issue9/quality-ratings/ [1999, January 11].

10. Anagnostelis, B. et al., "Thinking Critically about Information on the Web," *Vine*, 104, 1997, 21–8.

11. Brümmer, A., *Subject Based Information Gateways*, [online], 1998. Available: http://www.lub.lu.se/desire/sbigs.html [1999, January 11].

12. *Further Searching for Information on the Internet*, [online], 1998. Available: http://www.netskills.ac.uk/support/searching/search2.html [1999, January 11].

13. Bradley, P., *Multi-search Engines: A Comparison*, [online], 1998. Available: http://www.philb.com/msengine.htm [1999, January 11].

14. *Metacrawlers and Metasearch Engines*, [online], 1998. Available: http://searchenginewatch.com/facts/metacrawlers.html [1999, January 11].

3

Assessing the Quality of Any Internet Information Source

Chapter 1 provided an introduction to the concept of quality in relation to information which is available via the Internet. Chapter 2 examined the ever-increasing range of tools and facilities which are available for searching the Internet, focusing on possible strategies to assist users in looking for high-quality sources. This chapter is designed to help readers assess the quality of an information source once it has been located. It provides a detailed guide to those factors or characteristics which affect the quality, value, or usefulness of any information source which can be accessed via the Internet. However, as we have seen, any assessment of quality is dependent upon the needs of the individual seeking information, as well as on the nature of the source being evaluated. Therefore the criteria are not prescriptive, and readers should select the appropriate criteria depending upon the nature of the source and their particular needs.

The chapter is divided into ten areas of evaluation:

- identifying the purpose of a source
- assessing coverage
- assessing authority and reputation
- assessing accuracy
- assessing the currency and maintenance of a source
- considering the accessibility of a source
- evaluating the presentation and arrangement of information
- assessing how easy a source is to use
- making a comparison with other sources
- assessing the overall quality of a source.

Each section contains extensive notes on how to approach the particular aspect of evaluation, and examples are provided throughout. At the end of each section, a checklist is provided for easy reference.

Identifying the purpose of a source

The purpose of a source refers to its aims and objectives. These include the intended coverage, any stated limitations in the coverage (the scope), and the intended audience. Identifying the intended audience of a source or service is of particular importance, as a user will need to determine whether information is likely to be presented at a level which is suitable for his or her needs.

Evaluation will involve determining whether any aims, objectives, or limitations are stated within a source or service, and examining any such statements.

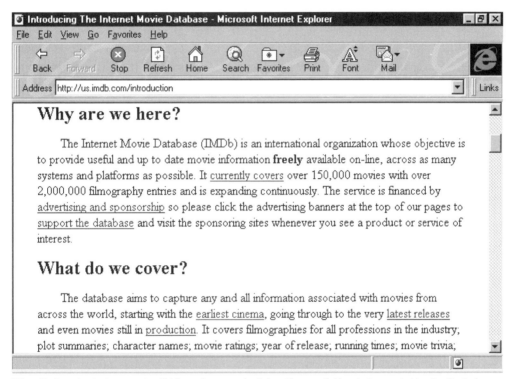

Fig. 3.1 *A statement of the aims and objectives of the Internet Movie Database. The Internet Movie Database is published by The Internet Movie Database Ltd.*

The *Internet Movie Database* (**http://us.imdb.com/**) is a well-known and widely used site which provides a searchable database of film information. A film and theater studies teacher might be interested in pointing her students towards this site for details of films, directors, and actors. Having heard about the site from another teacher, she would need to know whether it is suitable for her class. Two links are provided from the opening screen of the *Internet Movie Database* which are likely to provide useful information on its intended purpose. These are a link to "help" information and a link to "about" the site.

53

Following links such as these, or links entitled "frequently asked questions about this site," will often lead to details of the purpose of materials. In this instance, following the "about" link leads to a statement of the aims of the *Internet Movie Database*: "To provide useful and up-to-date movie information freely available online" (Figure 3.1). In addition, details of the intended coverage of the source are included: "The database aims to capture any and all information associated with movies from across the world," and covers "over 150,000 movies with over 2,000,000 filmography entries." Using this information, the teacher would be able to build a picture of the purpose of the site and make an assessment as to whether it will match the needs of her students.

Any assessment of purpose is inextricably linked to the other areas of evaluation which are discussed elsewhere in this chapter, particularly an assessment of coverage. By considering the other areas of assessment, it will be possible to determine whether the intended purpose has been achieved, whether the intended subject areas or materials are covered, and whether the information is appropriate for the intended audience.

CHECKLIST

Identifying the purpose of a source

☑ Is there a statement of the intended purpose of the source?

☑ Is there a statement of the aims, objectives, and intended coverage?

☑ What are the aims and objectives of the source?

☑ What is the intended coverage, and are there any limitations to it?

☑ Who are the intended audience?

Assessing coverage

The principal factor determining the usefulness of any information source is often the subject area covered, and the other factors described in this chapter are often of secondary importance. Factors affecting the coverage of a source are the subject areas and the types of materials covered, the comprehensiveness of coverage within a given area, the range of different subjects covered (the breadth), the level of detail provided about each subject (the depth), as well as any limitations to coverage (the scope). In addition, the retrospective coverage of a source or service (how far back in time material is covered) affects comprehensiveness and may therefore affect the value and usefulness of a source.

In order to assess coverage, evaluators will need to browse the source itself, or conduct a search for information on a topic with which they are familiar. They can then determine the comprehensiveness of coverage by considering whether all aspects of a subject have been covered which they would expect to be covered.

The teacher mentioned above might be interested in media portrayals of war. In order to evaluate the *Internet Movie Database*, a search could be conducted for war films. "War" as a keyword term retrieves 712 films. A knowledgeable user would be able to examine the films which are listed in order to assess the breadth of coverage (the range of different types of films which are included) and the comprehensiveness of coverage (whether all the films are included which they would expect). For example, films range from *When the Wind Blows*, an animated portrayal of the impact of nuclear war, to *Star Wars*. In addition, films are listed in different languages, and from different countries, and television series are also included. The dates of the films are recorded, including *Abraham Lincoln* from 1924, as well as many other films from the 1920s and 1930s, indicating that the retrospective coverage of the site is good. Moreover, a recently released film is retrieved, *Saving Private Ryan*, indicating the currency of the database (discussed further under "currency").

Level of detail for the intended audience

The level of detail or depth of coverage relates to the intended audience of a source. Users will need to evaluate whether a source provides sufficient information and whether the information is pitched at an appropriate level for their needs.

Figure 3.2 displays information from the *Culinary Connection* (**http://www.culinary.com/**), a site which provides news information relating to food issues, as well as access to hundreds of recipes. The screen shot displays one such news item relating to orange juice and prevention of heart disease. Users would need to consider whether enough information is provided for their needs – whether the level of detail is sufficient for them to assess the relationship between drinking two glasses of orange juice daily and the prevention of heart disease. Assessing whether information is pitched at an appropriate level involves reading through the text and attempting to determine whether it is either too sim-

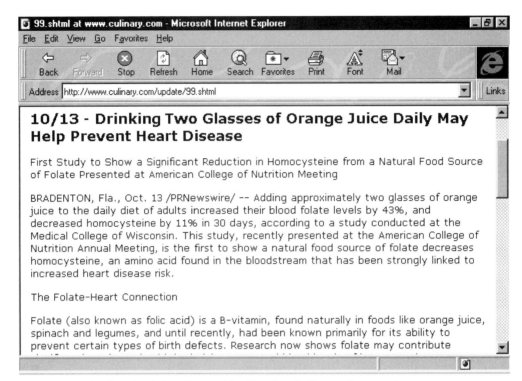

Fig. 3.2 *The level of detail provided in the Culinary Connection*

plistic or too complex. The text here might be considered too complex for a lay person, who is less likely to understand "blood folate levels" and "homocysteine," as well as the implications of the figures which are provided.

Pointers to further information

Pointers to further information, such as hypertext links to other sites or references to printed materials, can enhance the coverage of a source or service. The *Culinary Connection* mentioned above also includes extensive links to other resources of food-related information. Such links could also be evaluated by considering their coverage and whether they add value to the site itself. In this instance, a wide range of links are provided under various category headings, such as beverages (displayed in Figure 3.3), educational resources, chefs' pages, and organizations. Thus, the links provide access to a more extensive range of materials than is possible within the site itself. Furthermore, as displayed in Figure 3.3, there is some descriptive information about each link which adds value to them and enables users to select potentially relevant sites more easily. One further consideration is whether the links have been selected and on what basis. It is evident that these links have been selected on the basis of their rele-

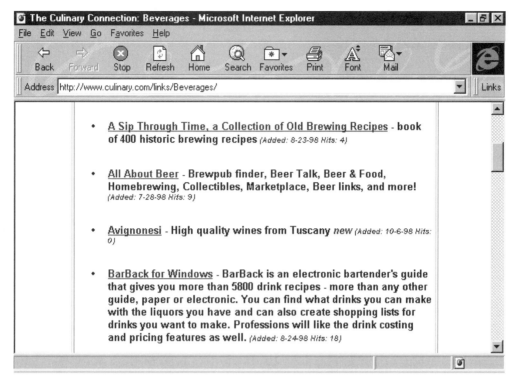

Fig. 3.3 *Links to further information from the Culinary Connection*

vance but unfortunately there is no information on whether they have been selected according to their quality.

Mirror sites

Some sites are "mirror sites" which, as their name suggests, are copies of an original site. Mirror sites are generally provided to enable faster access to materials (discussed further under "accessibility'), and both the mirror and the original site usually provide access to the same information. However, there may be local variations. For example, *AltaVista*, one of the general search engines discussed in Chapter 2, can be accessed via the original site in the USA (**http://www. altavista.com**), as well as via numerous other locations including Asia (**http://altavista.skali.com.my/**), Canada (**http://www.altavista-canada.com/**), and Australia (**http://www.altavista.yellowpages.com.au/**). These provide access to the same contents as the original USA location, but also include materials of regional interest. Thus, evaluators may need to consider whether they are using an original or a mirror site, whether they both cover the same materials, and the respective advantages and disadvantages of accessing the mirror versus the original site. In the example of *AltaVista*, information about the mirror sites is provided in the details about the service (**http://www. altavista.com/av/content/av_ network.html**).

CHECKLIST

Assessing coverage

☑ What subject areas and types of materials are covered by the source?

☑ What range of different subjects is covered?

☑ Are the subject areas covered comprehensively?

☑ What is the retrospective coverage of the source?

☑ What level of detail is provided, and is the level of detail sufficient for the audience? Is the information pitched at an appropriate level?

☑ Are there any pointers or links to further sources of information? Is any descriptive information available for any pointers or links? Are the pointers selected, and if so on what basis? Are the pointers valuable and useful?

☑ Is the site an original or a mirror site? Does the mirror site cover the same materials as the original? What are the advantages and disadvantages of accessing the mirror versus the original site?

Assessing authority and reputation

An assessment of the authority of an information source is based upon a range of factors, but primarily the knowledge and expertise of those responsible for producing it. A source is authoritative if it is written by a subject expert, or produced by an institution with recognized knowledge and expertise in the field. Authority is inextricably linked to reputation, including the reputation of the source itself, as well as the reputation of those responsible for producing the source. A good reputation is created because a source has been successful, useful or valuable on previous occasions, or because its author or institution are well-known for their knowledge and expertise in an area. The authority and reputation of a source affects the extent to which individuals will rely upon the information it contains, and therefore influences perceptions of its relative quality.

A number of techniques can be used to ascertain authority and reputation. For academic works, a literature search could be conducted to determine whether the author has published in the field before, and whether he or she has published in refereed journals. The expertise of an author may also be evaluated by determining whether she or he is a professional working in the field or just a lay person with a passing interest in the subject. Some sites include a statement of the experience of the authors, and this can be useful when attempting to make an assessment.

The proliferation of individuals publishing via the Internet means that many authors may be unknown, and the reputation of the institution is therefore of increased importance. Figure 3.4 is taken from the *Visible Human Project* (**http://www.nlm.nih.gov/research/visible/visible_human.html**), a project which is endeavoring to produce images of cross sections of the whole of the human body. The project is well-known within health care and medicine, and it is considered authoritative in part because it is produced by a reputable organization, namely the National Library of Medicine.

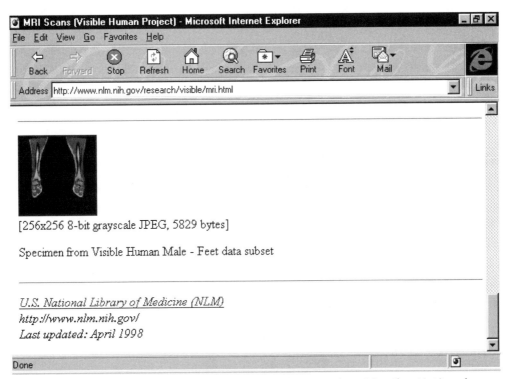

Fig. 3.4 *A page from the Visible Human Project produced by the National Library of Medicine displaying contact information, the site address, and an update date*

Alternatives to individual or institutional authority

It may be difficult to identify an individual or institution responsible for some sources. Under such circumstances, one consideration is the address of a source. For example, the first part of the site address for the *Visible Human Project* ends in ".gov," indicating that it is a government organization in the USA. The reputation and experience of any other organizations involved in the production of a source, such as publishers, sponsors, or funding agencies, can also indicate authority. Any reviews of a site or service can also provide an indication of the reputation and authority of sources, particularly if a review has been published in a well-respected journal within the field. One final consideration in assessing the reputation of a site is the use of counters – these often appear at the end of the first page of a site, and indicate how many people have visited the site during a specified time period. Thus, they can be used to assess a site's popularity. However, the use of counters has obvious limitations. A site's popularity does not necessarily equate with its quality, and counters include visitors to the first page of a site who may venture no further.

Some readers might consider authority and reputation too subjective to merit consideration. Furthermore, the assumption that the work of a reputable author or institution is likely to be of higher quality than those which are less well-known, is not always true. Reputations and expertise can change, and a newcomer to a field may be capable of producing high-quality work. Factors affecting source quality are not mutually exclusive, and authority and reputation must be considered in relation to, for example, the site's coverage, and the currency and accuracy of the information it contains.

Assessing accuracy

Accuracy generally refers to the factual accuracy or correctness of a source of information. However, the ease of assessing accuracy is affected both by the nature of the information and the expertise of the evaluator. For example, mathematical information is either correct or incorrect, but some theories are subjective and there may be no absolute right or wrong answer. Furthermore, some evaluators will be able to search a source for information about which they have some knowledge and expertise in order to make an assessment of accuracy, while others with little or no expertise might usefully conduct a search on a particular subject area and compare the results from different sources.

CHECKLIST

Assessing authority and reputation

☑ What is the reputation of the source? Is the source well-known?

☑ What is the reputation and experience of the author or institution responsible for the information? Is the source written by a subject expert or produced by an institution with recognized knowledge and expertise in the field?

☑ What is the reputation and experience of any other organizations involved in the production of the information, such as publishers, sponsors, or funding agencies?

☑ What is the address of the site? Does the address indicate an authoritative organization?

☑ Are there any reviews available discussing the source? Do they indicate that the site is reputable and authoritative? Are the reviews themselves authoritative?

☑ Is there a counter on the site? Does the number of visits to the site suggest that it is popular?

Beyond factual accuracy

There are numerous other factors which may affect the accuracy, as well as users' perceptions of the accuracy, of a source of information. These include: whether information has been through a refereeing or editing process; whether information is based upon research; the potential for bias introduced by authors, publishers, or sponsors (evaluators may wish to consider the motivation of those involved in the production of information); the availability of references to published information; and the professionalism or overall quality of a source, as indicated by spelling, grammatical, or typographical errors. Some sources provide a facility to send corrections to any inaccurate information, which is not only useful, but also suggests a concern for accuracy. Other related factors discussed elsewhere in this chapter include the authority and reputation of the source, the knowledge and expertise of the authors or organizations involved in producing the information, and the currency of the information.

As an example, a search for "nutrition," "sports," and "athletes" in *AltaVista* retrieves numerous hits. The first is "GU Sports Nutrition for Athletes and Athletic Training" (**http://www.gusports.com/index.html**), and the second, "Nutrition for Athletes" (**http://www.ausport.gov.au/nut.html**). Both sites sound potentially relevant. However, reading the first sentence in the search results which describes each site gives the user some insight into the likely accuracy of the information. The first begins, "GU, the country's best-selling energy gel, is the perfect sports nutrition product." The site sounds as though it is designed to advertise a product, and so any information is likely to be biased by a commercial imperative. In comparison, the description for the second site reads, "Nutrition for Athletes. Dr Louise Burke – Consultant Dietitian at the Australian Institute of Sport." This site is produced by an academic working at a reputable and authoritative-sounding institution, and it is therefore likely that the information provided here will be more accurate and less prone to bias. Furthermore, selecting the second site leads to detailed guidelines on nutrition for athletes with references to three sources of published information.

One reason for using the Internet is to find information about possible holiday destinations, and a wealth of resources is available on almost every

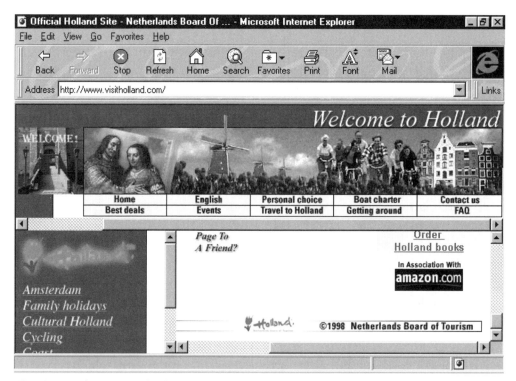

Fig. 3.5 *The copyright line provides an indication of authority for a Dutch tourist guide, "Welcome to Holland," produced by the Netherlands Board of Tourism*

possible location. It is important that details such as the dates of events or the opening times of museums are accurate. However, without making expensive telephone calls or learning through experience, it is almost impossible to check the accuracy of such information. The guide displayed in Figure 3.5 for Amsterdam and other Dutch locations is produced by the Netherlands Board of Tourism, as indicated at the bottom of the page (**http://www.visitholland.html**). Users are therefore given an indication of the authority of the source, and consequently the likelihood of the accuracy of the information.

CHECKLIST

Assessing accuracy

☑ Is the information contained in the source factually accurate?

☑ Are there any typographical, spelling, or grammatical errors?

☑ Is the information based on research or other evidence?

☑ Are there any references to published sources of information?

☑ Has the information been through any quality-control processes, such as refereeing or editing?

☑ Is the information likely to be biased by any individuals or organizations involved in its production? What is the motivation of those involved in the production of the source?

☑ Is there a facility to send corrections to inaccurate information?

Assessing the currency and maintenance of a source

The currency of a source relates to how up-to-date it is, and maintenance refers to whether a source is kept up-to-date. Currency and maintenance are central factors affecting use of the Internet to look for information, as there is a general perception that the Internet provides access to the most current information possible. Moreover, currency is an important consideration because outdated information can become useless, as well as inaccurate or misleading. However, currency will be of increased importance in relation to some sources and within some subject areas, while for others it may not require evaluation. For example, a ten-year-old tutorial on human anatomy may still be valuable, but a site providing access to news information will need to be frequently updated in order to ensure its accuracy.

Currency and maintenance are assessed by examining the date when any information was produced (either on the Internet or initially as a printed source), when the source was last updated, when it will next be updated, and the frequency of updating. Such details may be available from the source itself, such as an explicit statement of the date when the information was produced. In addition, there may be a statement of policy regarding the frequency of updating and the updating process.

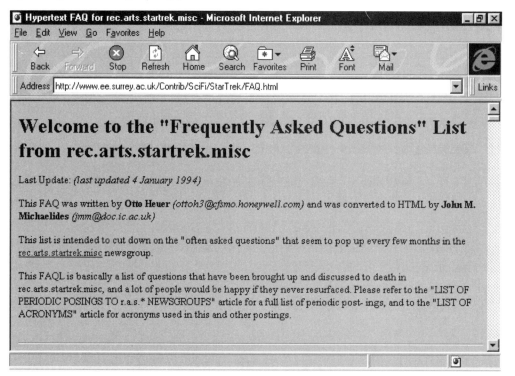

Fig. 3.6 *Star Trek FAQ*

Figure 3.4 includes a last update date for the *Visible Human Project*. The site was accessed in July 1998, and the date is April 1998, suggesting a current site. In contrast, Figure 3.6 displays an introduction to a Frequently Asked Questions (FAQ) file of information on Star Trek (**http://www.ee.surrey. ac.uk/Contrib/ SciFi/StarTrek/FAQ.html**) which was accessed at the same time but was last updated in January 1994. As mentioned, the importance of currency depends on the subject area and the nature of the source, and the significance of these dates will depend upon the need for current information and the potential impact of a four-year time-span on the accuracy of Star Trek information.

Sites may not explicitly state how frequently they are updated, they may not be as frequently updated as promised, and a "last update date" might only refer to parts of a site. Consequently, evaluators may need to search for current information. For example, the statement of coverage for the *Internet Movie Database* (Figure 3.1) claims that it covers "the very latest releases and even movies still in production," but is not explicit about the frequency of updating. Assessors could usefully search the database for any recently released films or for films which are still being produced – the example of *Saving Private Ryan* was mentioned earlier, a film which was only just released at the time of writing but included in the database. Evaluators might also need to monitor a source over time to ensure that it maintains the same level of currency.

Users could also browse through a source in order to gain an impression of whether it is generally well-maintained. Factors to consider include the currency of any hypertext links – the example was noted in Chapter 1 of a personal home page which included links to sites created by the author's friends which were no longer available. Indicators that sites are "under construction" may suggest the maintenance of a source, and users should consider returning to such sites at a later date for reassessment.

As mentioned, some materials include a policy regarding the updating process. Such a policy may include details of whether an individual or group is responsible for maintenance, their knowledge and expertise, and their motivation for doing so. If an individual or group maintains a site voluntarily, they may be more likely to lose interest and therefore not maintain the site effectively in the long term. Contact information for site maintainers is also a useful feature and suggests a concern for site maintenance.

Considering the accessibility of a source

Generally, the main factor determining whether a source of information is accessed and used is the subject area covered. However, accessibility can affect the choice of the sources to be used, whether once only or regularly. The Internet is frequently used because it is convenient, networked computers are easily accessible, and it is faster and easier than going to a library. In addition, the Internet is often used because people are loathe to pay high prices for information from other places. Consequently, Internet users will generally want to access information as quickly, as cheaply, and as easily as possible.

CHECKLIST

Assessing the currency and maintenance of a source

☑ Is there an explicit date for the information? When was the source originally produced, either in printed form or on the Internet?

☑ Is the information up-to-date? When was the information last updated? When will the information next be updated? How frequently is the information updated?

☑ Is there a statement of policy regarding the frequency of updating and the updating process?

☑ Is the site generally well-maintained? Are any links to external sources up-to-date?

☑ Is there a maintenance policy?

☑ Is there an individual or group responsible for maintenance? Do they maintain the site voluntarily? What is their knowledge and expertise?

☑ Are contact details available for a site maintainer?

☑ Is there any indication that the source is "under construction"?

☑ Does the source need to be monitored or reassessed at a later date to ensure continued currency and maintenance?

Speed of access

There are a wide range of factors which affect the ease with which sources may be accessed. Speed of access is of particular concern, and factors affecting speed include the location of the sources, the number and size of any images, and whether thumbnail images have been used to improve access speeds. The image displayed in Figure 3.4 is a thumbnail, a small image which can be selected to display a much larger graphic. This enables the page to download much more quickly than if the full-sized images had been used, and the users can subsequently decide whether they want to wait to view particular pictures in more detail. The availability of a mirror site can also enable faster access. As mentioned, *AltaVista*, one of the general search engines discussed in Chapter 2, can be accessed via the original site in the USA, as well as via numerous other locations including Asia, Canada, and Australia. Individuals in these locations are likely to access *AltaVista* much faster using one of the local mirror sites than if they use the original site in the USA.

Software restrictions

A further consideration is the mode or modes of access available – whether sites are only available using multimedia WWW browsers, such as *Internet Explorer* or *Netscape Navigator*, or whether they are also accessible using a text browser, or via FTP or Telnet. Sites are generally slower to access using multimedia browsers, and a site which is limited to these will also exclude users with only basic facilities for accessing the Internet. Again using the example of *AltaVista*, the default graphical page includes a link to a "text-only version" (**http://www. altavista.com/cgi-bin/query?text**) which downloads much more quickly.

Specific software or hardware may also be required to access the full "bells and whistles" version of some information. For example, certain journals and magazines rely on PDF in order to display articles in a high-quality presentation format. PDF, Portable Document Format, is a file format developed by Adobe Systems[1] for use with its Acrobat Reader. PDF documents can be displayed and printed in a form which is virtually identical to an original paper-based publication, and this enables the use of more sophisticated text and graphics formats than is possible using HTML. Figure 3.7 is an example of a report displayed in PDF format using the Acrobat Reader. Where software is required, it should be easily accessible (there should be a link to a relevant site for downloading the software), and instructions should be available for downloading and using the software.

Other access restrictions

Access to various sources via the Internet may be restricted by the language used, the need for registration (which can be a cumbersome process) or a password, or the need to prove eligibility or membership of a particular organization. Individuals are required to remember so many passwords that some sources enable people to bookmark pages to avoid the need to reenter their password each time they use the site, and others provide a route for those who have forgotten their passwords. Cookies are a relatively new facility. These allow individual users to specify certain preferences when viewing particular WWW sites and pages. The user must enable the feature,[2] and the user's WWW browser then allocates space on the hard drive where the preferences (or cookies) are stored. Each time the user visits a particular site, the browser checks to

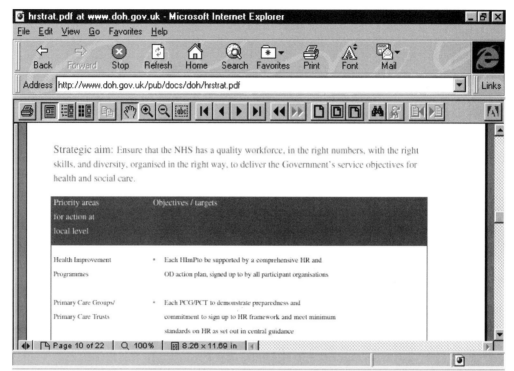

Fig. 3.7 *Document displayed in PDF format using the Acrobat reader plug-in. "Working together: Securing a quality workforce for the National Health Service," Department of Health. Crown copyright, reproduced with the permission of the Controller of Her Majesty's Stationery Office.*

see if there are any predefined cookies for that site, and if there are, the cookie is sent to the server along with the request for the page concerned. Cookies can be used, for example, for storing usernames and passwords, or for storing account numbers for sites which charge for viewing.

The Lancet (**http://www.thelancet.com/**) is a high-quality medical journal which has been available for many years as a paper-based publication. The opening page, displayed in Figure 3.8, provides an access route for first-time users who must register to use the site, a route for those subscribed to the printed journal, and access to a limited range of services for those who have already registered to use the site. Clicking on the first option leads to an electronic registration form which requests some personal information and includes an easily completed questionnaire. The user then selects a username and password, and is now able to access the whole site (if he or she subscribes to the paper-based journal) or parts of the site (if not a subscriber). Thus registration is a fairly straightforward process. Moreover, once the registration form has been completed, those users who have enabled the cookies facility on their own machine can select the appropriate link from the page displayed in Figure 3.8 and their username and password are automatically input for them.

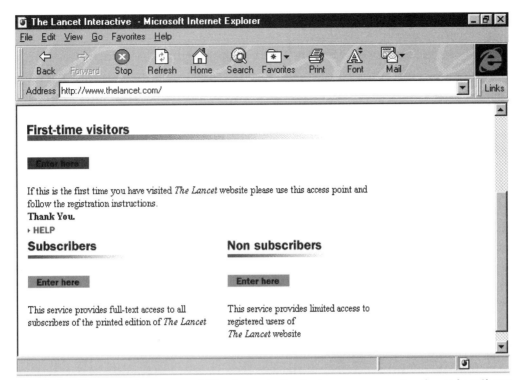

Fig. 3.8 *The opening page of The Lancet displaying access routes for subscribers and nonsubscribers to the journal. © by The Lancet Ltd, 1998*

Cost

Cost will obviously be a consideration in the use of sources. Evaluators will need to identify whether there is a charge for accessing information, and what charging schemes are available, as well as whether it is possible to view some information for free. As mentioned, *The Lancet* provides two options for users, "full-text access to all subscribers of the printed edition" and "limited access to registered users of *The Lancet* website" (Figure 3.8). An evaluator would need to determine the cost of the journal, how much information is freely available, and the value and usefulness of any free information in comparison with the original publication. There is a link from the opening screen of the journal to "About *The Lancet* Interactive," which includes details of what information is available for free (the contents listings plus some articles), and what additional facilities are available (e.g., access to discussion about articles which have appeared online, and a search facility). In addition, some services charge for accessing an electronic version of paper-based materials, and assessors might need to consider the relative value of paying to access the electronic version. Under certain circumstances, a user might also wish to consider the cost of one source in comparison with another which provides access to similar information (this is discussed further under "making a comparison with other sources").

Copyright

A further consideration is the availability of copyright information. Users will sometimes want to reuse textual and graphical materials, such as in a publication or presentation. Copyright law relating to the use of electronic information, and information available via the Internet in particular, varies from country to country. However, as a basic rule, any information which is obtained via the Internet will be covered by copyright, including images, the text of WWW pages, and the contents of e-mail and Usenet messages. It is therefore useful if authors provide a statement of the copyright ownership of materials, and details of how materials should be cited in a publication or attributed to an author, as well as details of who should be contacted when copyright permission is required.

Reliability of access and ease of finding sources

Another issue is the reliability of access. Some sites are unavailable at particular times of the day, often due to site maintenance or updating. Where applicable, such times should be specified in the details about the site, and the amount of downtime should be kept to a minimum.

There are also a number of factors relating to the ease of locating resources. For example, some sites frequently move, and some fail to provide a link to their new location. The use of metadata can make it easier to find resources. As mentioned in Chapter 2, metadata is data about data, similar to a bibliographical record, which is written into the HTML of a WWW page itself. Some search engines, such as *AltaVista*, now use metadata where available in order to create resource descriptions and index pages, thus ensuring more effective retrieval and description.

Evaluating the presentation and arrangement of information

As with accessibility, the presentation and arrangement of information is generally secondary to its content. Most Internet users are primarily concerned with the information contained in a source, and will use it regardless of how the information has been presented. In addition, the presentation and arrangement of information is a matter of personal taste: one person will feel a particular feature is essential while another feels the same feature is redundant. Assessment also tends to rely on an individual's general impressions of whether there is a good overall design and whether the source is professionally presented.

CHECKLIST

Considering the accessibility of a source

☑ Is the source fast to access?

☑ Does the location affect the speed of access?

☑ Have thumbnail images been used to improve access speeds?

☑ Is there a local mirror site?

☑ What mode(s) of access are available? Does the mode of access affect the speed?

☑ Is any additional software or hardware required? Is any additional software easily accessible, and are instructions available from the original source for downloading and using the software?

☑ Are there any restrictions to access, such as registration, passwords, proof of eligibility, or membership of an organization? Is registration straightforward? Is it possible to bookmark a page, or have cookies been used, to avoid the need to reenter passwords? Is there a route for users who have forgotten their passwords?

☑ What language is the information in?

☑ Does it cost anything to access the source? What charging schemes are available? Is some information available for free? How useful and valuable is the free information in comparison with what is charged for?

☑ Is there a statement of copyright ownership? Are there details of how materials should be cited in a publication or attributed to an author? Is contact information available?

☑ Is the source reliably accessible, or is it frequently unavailable? Are the times specified when the site is unavailable?

☑ Is the site stable, or does it frequently move location? If the site moves, is forwarding information provided?

☑ Has metadata been used in the authoring of materials to ensure effective indexing and retrieval by search engines?

Browsing through a source will enable the evaluator to build such an overall impression, and to consider whether the source is clearly, consistently and logically presented and arranged. However, some users will have a specific interest in the presentation of materials, and presentation can also influence the ease of finding and using information within a source. Resources therefore need to be judged accordingly.

Aids to finding information within a source

Features such as a site map, contents list, index, menu system, or search facility will be beneficial in helping users to find the information they are looking for, as well as in familiarizing themselves with the materials which are available in a source. Evaluators would need to try using any such features to find information within a source in order to assess their effectiveness. Where categories have been used to organize information, evaluators should assess whether the information has been appropriately and usefully organized.

Further considerations include the number of "clicks" required to locate relevant information, whether steps are unnecessarily repeated, and whether useful "shortcuts" are available, such as a "home" icon to take users directly to the start of a document or resource. In addition, some WWW pages are extremely long, and users must painstakingly scroll through them to find what they want. Alternatives include providing links between different sections of the same page, or splitting a page in two and providing links between them. Conversely, some authors create separate pages for small sections of the same document, forcing the user to download many different short sections without offering the option to scroll through larger sections. Obviously, the length of a page is a highly subjective issue, but evaluators should consider whether a useful balance has been achieved and whether the organization of the material into sections is appropriate.

The presentation and arrangement of information on the screen can influence the ease of assimilating the information. This includes whether screens are clearly laid out and aesthetically pleasing, whether there is too much information on each screen, whether the text is easy to read and whether headings stand out. Moreover, a well-written source in a clear style is much easier to take in than an obscure, verbose one.

The presentation of hypertext links, and how a link is defined and included in the text, can also help or hinder access to the information. Different authors present hypertext links in different ways. One option is to be explicit and include text such as "Click here for . . ." or "This is a link to . . . ," and another is simply to use an appropriate word without interrupting the flow of the text (this assumes that because hypertext links are usually in a different color and underlined it is self-evident what they are). A third alternative is to use the URL (the address) of the site which is linked to. For example, *Lycos Top 5%* has used the first option (Figure 2.6), the *Internet Movie Database*, the second (Figure 3.1), and *SOSIG*, the third (Figure 2.7). Whatever approach has been used, evaluators will need to consider whether the hypertext links are meaningful (is it obvious from the link what is being pointed to?), and whether the presentation of the links interrupts the user's reading of the information.

In order to illustrate some of the above issues, Figures 3.9 and 3.10 display two screens from the *BUBL Information Service* (one of the virtual libraries described in the previous chapter). The opening screen (Figure 3.9) is clearly laid out, as all the links are easily displayed on one screen. It is possible to navigate from here to any of the major sections of the service, and the resources which are linked to from each hypertext link are self-evident. Figure 3.10 displays the options for accessing information within *BUBL Link*. Several links are available (searching, browsing by Dewey Class, browsing by subject, or random browsing), providing a range of options to facilitate information access. Evaluators could attempt to locate information using these tools in order to determine their effectiveness. The hypertext links are self-evident, and

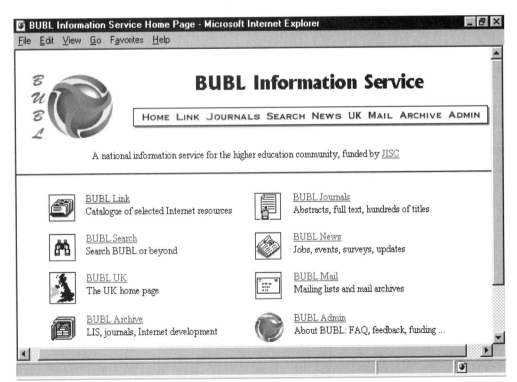

Fig. 3.9 *The opening page of the BUBL Information Service*

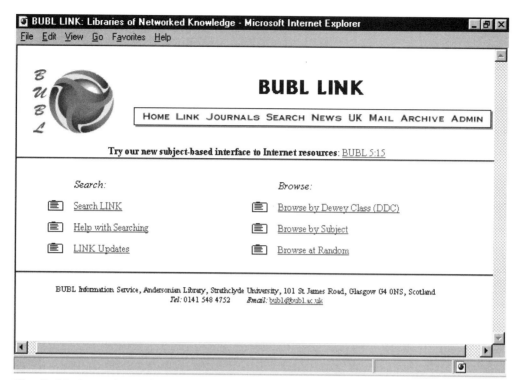

Fig. 3.10 *Accessing information in the BUBL Information Service*

comparison of the two screens highlights the consistency in presentation and arrangement throughout the source which helps the user to find his or her way around the material.

Images, frames, Java . . .

Some individuals prefer simplicity in presentation, while others favor the use of frames, graphics, and moving images or text. Moving images or text can be created using Java (a programming language) or Javascript and Dynamic HTML. Frames are used to break a screen up into two or more sub-pages, allowing a site producer to display more than one page at the same time. A popular use of frames is to display the contents listing for a site in one frame, while the user simultaneously views individual pages within the site in a second frame. An example of this is displayed in Figure 4.9 – the contents of the site are displayed in the left-hand frame, with the selected page displayed on the right. The user can browse the right-hand frame without affecting the contents listing on the left.

Under certain circumstances, the use of frames, graphics, and moving images can add value to a source. Figure 3.11 displays the opening screen to *Yahooligans!* (**http://www.yahooligans.com/**), a search tool designed specifically for

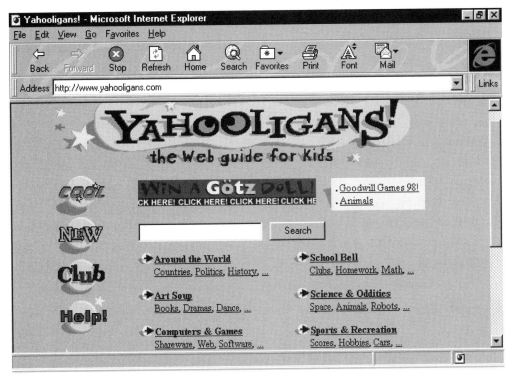

Fig. 3.11 *Opening screen for the Yahooligans! search tool. Text and artwork copyright © 1998 by Yahoo! Inc. All rights reserved. YAHOO! and the YAHOO! logo are trademarks of YAHOO! Inc.*

children. The opening screen includes far more graphics than the opening screen to *BUBL* (Figure 3.9), because the service is designed to attract younger users. However, as mentioned under "accessibility," the use of such features can reduce access speeds, and may also be offputting to some people. Evaluators should therefore assess whether such features have been used appropriately, whether they are necessary and add value to a source, or whether they do little more than slow down access. It could be argued that graphics are necessary here because of the intended audience, while in a service such as *BUBL* they would be superfluous. Another issue is the location of graphics or images in relation to the text. Obviously graphics should be placed near to the text to which they relate, or else appropriate referencing should be used to signpost the reader.

A related factor is whether pages are also available in a text-only version, or whether they still work without graphics. As mentioned under "accessibility," the number and size of images can affect access speeds, and therefore many users choose to view materials with the "show pictures" option of their browser turned off to speed up downloading. It is possible for WWW authors to specify text which is displayed as an alternative to an image (this is usually a brief description of the image concerned), as well as to offer a "no frames" option for viewing pages. These alternatives ensure that pages are meaningful to any user, irrespective of the browser used or whether images are being viewed.

A further issue is advertising. Initially, many Internet users were strongly opposed to the use of advertising when it first started appearing on Internet-based materials. As advertising has become much more widespread, its use is generally accepted (or at least tolerated). However, advertising should still be used appropriately and it should not detract from the information itself. For example, the advertisement displayed on the opening screen of *Yahooligans!* does not overpower the screen, nor does it draw the user away from the basic function of the page, to search or browse *Yahooligans!*. If users are interested in more detail about the product being advertised, they can opt to click on the advertisement.

Assessing how easy a source is to use

Generally evaluators will build up an overall impression of whether they feel a source is easy to use while actually using it in order to investigate the other criteria which have already been discussed. Moreover, the factors affecting ease of use are inextricably linked to the accessibility of sources, as well as to the presentation and arrangement of information. Sources should be easy to access, it should be easy to move around a source and locate information, and any searching or browsing facilities should be straightforward and easy to use. A specific consideration is whether sites are intuitive and user-friendly, or whether training or familiarity are required before a site can be used effectively.

User support services

User support services can make it easier to use the materials. Examples include help information, training courses, telephone helplines, and contact information. Evaluators should appraise the value and usefulness of any user support, including the level of detail of help information, whether it is clear, and whether it is context-sensitive (i.e., different help is available according to the point the user is at in using the source). Other considerations are the meaningfulness of system messages, the response times for telephone helplines, and whether there is any response to e-mails or telephone messages.

The BIDS service (**http://www.bids.ac.uk/websearch.html**) provides access to a range of bibliographical databases, including the ISI *Citation Indexes*, *Embase*, and *ERIC*. Such services must be easy to use if they are to be used effectively. Initially the Internet version of the *Citation Indexes* was only accessible

CHECKLIST

Evaluating the presentation and arrangement of information

☑ Is the source clearly presented and arranged?

☑ Is the source logically presented and arranged?

☑ Is the presentation and arrangement of each page consistent throughout the source?

☑ Is there a site map, contents list, index, menu system, or search facility? Are any such facilities effective?

☑ Is the information categorized, and has it been appropriately organized?

☑ Are individual pages within a site appropriately divided up? Are there too few long pages or too many short pages?

☑ Are steps unnecessarily repeated? Are shortcuts available to access information in as few clicks as possible?

☑ Are individual screens clear and aesthetically pleasing?

☑ Is the text easy to read? Do headings stand out?

☑ Is the source well-written?

☑ How are hypertext links defined? Are they meaningful? Do they interrupt the flow of the text?

☑ Are there any graphics or moving images? Are they necessary? Have they been used appropriately? Do they add value to the text? Are they logically presented in relation to the text? Is a text-only version of the source available?

☑ Have frames been used? Are they necessary? Have they been used appropriately? Do they add value to the text? Is it possible to view the pages without frames?

☑ Are there any advertisements? Have they been used appropriately, or do they distract the user from the information or the main purpose of the page?

```
BIDS ISI Help
----------------------------------------------------------------------
AUTHOR NAME
----------------------------------------------------------------------


In the Author field, search expressions can be a single term (author name) or several terms connected
by one or more of the following operators:

•plus (+) or ampersand (&) for logical AND
•comma (,) for logical OR
•minus (-) for logical NOT


The format of author names is SURNAME_INITIALS (up to 5 initials are allowed), eg: BROWN_RSJ

Truncation
You can use an asterisk (*) for right-hand truncation in the author name expression, eg:

•BROWN_RA* will match BROWN_RA, BROWN_RAB, etc
•BROWN_R* will match BROWN_R, BROWN_RB, BROWN_RXZ, etc
•BROWN_* or BROWN_ or BROWN will match BROWN with any initials
•BROWN* will match BROWN and other names such as BROWNE, BROWNING, etc


Omit hyphens, apostrophes, diacritical marks, etc.

•DABO_J will find J D'Abo
•MORGANJONES_K will find K Morgan-Jones


Join up compound names, eg:

•VANDENBERG_WJ will find W J Van den Berg


For names that do not conform to the usual forename-surname pattern, treat the last as the surname and
use the first letter of each preceding name as an initial, eg:

MINH_HC for Ho Chi Minh.

Omit titles and generational qualifiers such as Professor, Junior etc.

----------------------------------------------------------------------
Use your browser's Back button to exit Help and return to the previous page.
----------------------------------------------------------------------

You can phone the BIDS Help Desk on +44 (0)1225 826074, or e-mail the Help Desk at
bidshelp@bids.ac.uk. If you're using your own terminal (not a public one, in the library, for example)
you can probably e-mail us by clicking here.
```

Fig. 3.12 *Help and user support details for an author search in the BIDS ISI databases*

via a Telnet service which was confusing to new users and required some degree of familiarity before it could be used effectively. The service is now also available via a WWW interface. The opening screen includes query input boxes for keyword and author searching. At the top of each screen there is a link to general help information, and underneath each search option, certain words such as "title/keyword/abstract" and "author," are underlined and displayed in a different color, denoting hypertext links. Following any of these links leads the user to detailed, context-sensitive help information – the details provided about author searching are displayed in Figure 3.12. This help information is fairly clear and useful, providing examples of how to conduct an author search, how to broaden a search, and how to search for more than one author. At the bottom of the screen, details of user support services (a helpdesk telephone number and e-mail address) are included, and this information is available from every screen within the service. Evaluators would need to assess these services in terms of the response times and the helpfulness of any responses.

CHECKLIST

Assessing how easy a source is to use

☑ Is the source generally easy to use?

☑ Is the source user-friendly and intuitive, or are training and/or experience required in order to use the source effectively?

☑ Is the source easy to access?

☑ Is it easy to move around the source and locate information?

☑ Are any searching or browsing facilities straightforward and easy to use?

☑ Is any help information available? Is the help information clear? Is the help information sufficient? Is the help information context sensitive? Is the help information valuable and useful?

☑ Are any system messages meaningful and useful?

☑ Are any training courses available? Is there a telephone helpline? Are any other user support services available? Is there any contact information?

☑ Is the user support valuable and useful? Is there any response to e-mails or telephone messages, and is the response time acceptable?

Making a comparison with other sources

In any assessment of the quality of a source, it is essential to determine its value in relation to others that are available. All the criteria and evaluation details which have been discussed already in this chapter could be used as points of comparison: sites might be compared in terms of their purpose, coverage, authority and reputation, accuracy, currency and maintenance, accessibility, presentation, and ease of use. Evaluators will find they automatically draw comparisons between different sources in order to decide which is the best to use under certain circumstances. This is likely to occur, not only when evaluating materials, but also while looking at search results and while using different sites and services. Some comparisons have already been drawn in this chapter between different sites and services. For example, while looking at the results for a search on sports, athletes and nutrition, a comparison was drawn between the likely accuracy of two different sources. Comparisons have also been drawn between the currency of different materials, and how different WWW pages are presented.

In order to illustrate this area of assessment further, Figures 3.13 and 3.14 display the opening screens from two job vacancies services, *jobs.ac.uk* (**http://www.jobs.ac.uk/**) and the *NISS Vacancies* service (**http://www.vacan-**

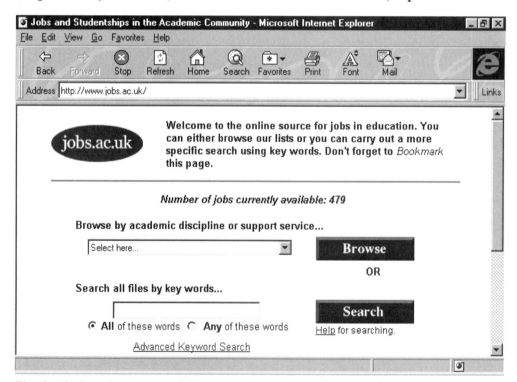

Fig. 3.13 *Opening screen of the vacancies service, jobs.ac.uk*

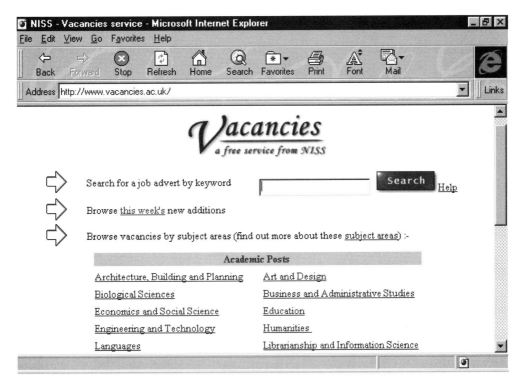

Fig. 3.14 *Opening screen of the NISS Vacancies service*

cies.ac.uk/). These services are broadly similar in terms of the subject areas covered – they both provide details of jobs within the UK higher education sector. In addition, they both provide keyword searching and browsing facilities, the categories of job advertisements are broadly similar, and the jobs advertised are submitted by users, which determines the amount of information provided about each job. Both are produced by authoritative organizations, the services appear to be maintained daily (each job advertisement includes a date when it was added), and contact information and copyright details are included in both. Furthermore, both sites are clearly laid out and easy to use, and the job advertisements themselves are reached in the same number of clicks (by browsing on the subject category, a list of brief descriptions are displayed which link to the full advertisement).

However, there are some differences between the two services which evaluators would need to consider in order to decide which to use or to recommend to others, bearing in mind the needs of the user. For example, *jobs.ac.uk* provides links to other sources of job information; while the links are not extensive, they do enhance the coverage of the service. The *NISS* service includes a link at the top of the opening screen (shown in Figure 3.14) to browse the week's new additions. Although this particular option is not available via *jobs.ac.uk*, it is possible to have new advertisements e-mailed every Saturday morning, an option which some might feel is preferable as they would not need to remember to access the WWW site each week. Other differences include an advanced search option and help information in *jobs.ac.uk*.

Comparative costs and value for money

Evaluators will also need to assess the comparative cost of sources and their relative value for money. In addition, the potential extra benefits offered by accessing information via the Internet should be considered where information is also available in other formats. For example, the electronic version of *The Lancet* might be compared with the paper-based version. Value-added features of the electronic version include the ability to e-mail comments on articles, and a search facility, but a paper-based copy of the journal is obviously more portable and might be considered easier to browse through.

Uniqueness

Evaluators should attempt to determine whether a source provides coverage of a subject which no other sources offer, whether a source has any unique features or facilities, and whether a source provides access to information in a unique format. For example, the *Visible Human Project* (mentioned earlier) is unique in its attempt to provide images of cross-sections of the whole of the human body. Sources which are unique in some way are likely to be used regardless of their other attributes and characteristics if it is the unique feature which a user is particularly interested in.

Assessing the overall quality of a source

A final stage in evaluating any source of information must be to take a step back and consider the overall impression which the source has given. An overall impression is generally based upon perceptions or experiences of the value and usefulness of a source, or of the information it contains, and such an impression is developed through familiarity or extensive and frequent use. Evaluators will also begin to create an overall opinion of any sources they assess, and they will start to draw conclusions about materials after considering the various criteria described in this chapter, such as that one source is "excellent" and "outstanding," while another is "not very interesting," or another is "rubbish."

CHECKLIST

Making a comparison with other sources

☑ Is the source unique in terms of its content or format, or does the source offer any unique features or facilities?

☑ What is the purpose of the source compared with others?

☑ What is the coverage of the source compared with others?

☑ How authoritative and reputable is the source compared with others?

☑ How accurate is the source compared with others?

☑ How current and well-maintained is the source compared with others?

☑ How accessible is the source compared with others?

☑ Is the information contained in the source well-presented and arranged compared with others?

☑ How easy is the source to use compared with others?

☑ What are the benefits of accessing this information via the Internet compared with other formats?

☑ What is the cost of the source and its value for money in comparison with others?

Reviews and recommendations

Those involved in selection and evaluation will rarely have the time or resources to use a site extensively or to consider every evaluative issue mentioned in this chapter. Therefore, two useful sources of further advice are reviews and recommendations from other users. A wide range of different journals and magazines provide reviews of WWW sites and other Internet materials. For example, the "OnLine" section of the *Guardian* newspaper includes reviews of various materials, and other newspapers also offer similar guides. In addition, the previous chapter discussed a range of virtual libraries and subject-based gateway services as well as popular rating and reviewing sites. These could be consulted, first to determine whether a site is included in any appropriate databases of quality materials, and second to consult any available reviews. Users might also be able to elicit the comments of friends or colleagues who have already used a site, or have been using a site extensively over a period of time.

By examining reviews and recommendations, the evaluator is provided with an indication of someone else's overall impression of the quality, value, and usefulness of a source. Caution is needed, however, because sites can change and resources might require reassessment. Furthermore, different materials are used for different reasons, and one person's assessment of quality might not be the same as another's.

CHECKLIST

Assessing the overall quality of a source

☑ What is the overall assessment of the source? What conclusions can be drawn after considering the evaluation issues discussed in this chapter? Is the source valuable and useful, and is the information contained in the source valuable and useful?

☑ Are any reviews available?

☑ Is the site included in any databases of high-quality materials, or has the site been reviewed by a rating or reviewing service?

☑ Is it possible to elicit comments from people who have used the source or who use it regularly? what is their overall impression of the source?

References

1. *Adobe*, [online], 1998. Available: **http://www.adobe.com/** [1999, January 11].
2. For more information on this process, see *Persistent Client State http Cookies: Preliminary Specification – Use with Caution*, [online], 1998. Available: **http://home.netscape.com/newsref/std/cookie_spec.html** [1999, January 11].

4

Evaluating Particular Types of Sources

Chapter 3 examined ten areas of assessment which relate to the evaluation of any source of information which is available via the Internet. However, a wide range of types of sources are now available, and different people access and use these for different reasons. Consequently, users are often interested in specific quality issues. For example, a user of a personal home page might be more concerned with the authority of the information, while a user of an FTP archive might wish to assess access speeds. This chapter provides details of the factors to consider when evaluating specific types of sources.

The source types can be divided up as follows:

- organizational WWW sites
- personal home pages
- subject-based WWW sites
- electronic journals and magazines
- image-based and multimedia sources
- Usenet newsgroups and discussion lists
- databases
- FTP archives
- Current awareness services
- FAQs.

Each source type is defined, the various factors which might be considered during an assessment of each source type are explained, and a worked example is provided in order to illustrate the points. In addition, each section includes a checklist of the assessment factors relevant to the source type.

Chapter 3 provides a detailed guide to those factors which affect the quality of any information source available via the Internet. Many of the factors discussed in Chapter 3 are applicable to the sources discussed here, and to avoid repetition, these have not been repeated. Readers are referred in this chapter to the appropriate sections from Chapter 3, and the examples have been used to illustrate how the generic criteria can be applied when evaluating specific source types. If a particular source does not fit into any of the ten categories, readers should again apply the generic criteria.

As has frequently been mentioned, any assessment of quality depends on the needs of the individual seeking information as well as on the nature of the source being evaluated. Therefore, the criteria relating to each source type are not prescriptive and readers should select the appropriate criteria depending upon the nature of the source and their particular needs.

Organizational WWW sites

"Organizational WWW sites" refers to a collection of WWW pages which are created and maintained by a particular organization. These include company and university sites, the site of a professional group, and of any other society or organization. The example provided in this section is the WWW site for the US National Gallery of Art.

Often organizational sites include personal home pages which are created and maintained by individuals working or associated with the organization concerned, and many organizational sites include extensive materials relating to subject areas of interest to them. Both personal home pages and subject-based WWW sites are discussed later in this chapter.

Assessing organizational WWW sites

Individuals often access the home page of a particular organization because they are interested in facts relating to it, such as an address or a phone number. Therefore, it is essential that basic factual information pertaining to the organization (e.g., phone number, address, e-mail address, opening times, etc.) is available and easy to locate within the site. Some sites provide little more than this basic information, while others provide detailed information about the organization or institution, as well as links to related sites and services which are of interest to potential users. Consequently, evaluators may want to focus on the coverage of sites, and whether sufficient information is provided for the user.

Other areas of assessment include:

- authority and reputation: in making an assessment, the expertise, and reputation of the institution within its field is obviously going to be of importance

■ currency and maintenance: materials must be maintained, as outdated information about an organization will become inaccurate and unreliable. While it is not usually necessary to maintain information about an organization on a very frequent basis, such as daily or weekly, it is essential that the user can determine when the materials were last updated in order to estimate their likely accuracy. Therefore, each page should include the date when it was last updated.

While the above factors are likely to be of major concern when evaluating organizational sites, almost all of the generic criteria discussed in Chapter 3 are applicable to this source type.

EXAMPLE

Evaluating the US National Gallery of Art WWW site

Like many art galleries and museums throughout the world, the US National Gallery of Art has now developed its own WWW site (**http://www.nga. gov/home.htm**).

Coverage

From the opening screen of the National Gallery site, various links are displayed, including links to help information, a search facility for the site, general information, information on collections and exhibitions, details of programs and events, and a link to "the shop." Obviously users interested in the opening times of the gallery would follow the link to "general information," where they will find the location and opening hours of the gallery, entry fees (the gallery is free), and a calendar of events. There are also details about the gallery itself and a brief history. While there is no date on these pages, the currency of the material is evident as the events listed in the calendar are for the current month. Indeed, the calendar is a valuable feature for anyone interested in visiting Washington and considering a trip to the gallery – events are listed by date, with the type of event (e.g., lectures, films, or slide shows), the times, the title, and a link to information about each event.

The links from the opening screen include "highlights" and "the Van Gogh exhibition." Details include the opening times and information on the paintings to be displayed (Figure 4.1), as well as an option to view a virtual tour of the

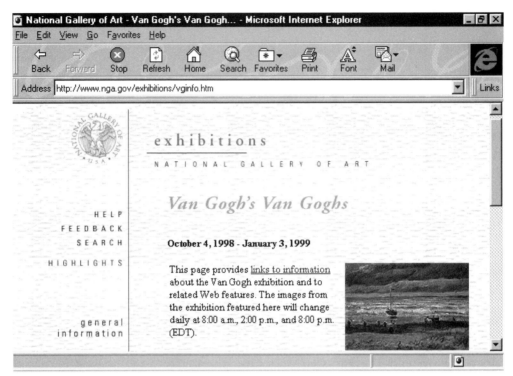

Fig. 4.1 *Details of the Van Gogh exhibition at the National Gallery of Art, Washington*

exhibition – this would be an excellent facility for a Van Gogh fan located elsewhere in the world.

Indeed, by examining the material about the various exhibitions and collections, evaluators are able to establish that this site provides access to far more than simply facts about the organization itself. Following the links to "collections" from the opening screen leads to a range of options, including "Dutch and Flemish painting of the 16th and 17th centuries," followed by a link to "Dutch landscapes and seascapes." The user is presented with six thumbnail images and an overview of this collection. The images can be viewed in full, and there is detailed information about each painting, as well as a bibliography of published references. This site could evidently be of value to an art student, critic, or historian as well as to those interested in visiting the gallery, and the authority of the information is assured in that the provider is a prestigious organization. Moreover, the provision of published references adds further weight to the accuracy of the information.

Evaluators are able to determine the coverage of the site by examining the "help" option, which includes indicators of what information is located where, how to find materials, and how to use the search facility.

Overall impression

Therefore, an overall impression of this site must be that it not only supplies useful and up-to-date information about the gallery itself, but that it is also a valuable source of material on various aspects of art and painting. However, there are some drawbacks to the site, notably the speed of access. This may be because the evaluation was conducted in the UK during the afternoon, a time which is notoriously slow for accessing sites in the US. In an effort to improve the speed of downloading materials, the option to view images was turned off. However, the site developers have not used text to indicate the content of the images, and certain pages are meaningless without graphics, especially where images have been used to replace menu options. While these issues do not directly influence the quality of the information, they will impact upon the ease of accessing and browsing the site.

Personal home pages

A personal home page is a WWW page, or a collection of pages, which is maintained by an individual and which relates to his or her personal interests. Personal home pages often include materials relating to a specific subject area, and may be part of a wider organizational WWW site. Where readers are interested in the subject focus of a personal home page, they are recommended also to read the section on "subject-based WWW pages." Likewise, those interested in evaluating the wider organizational site should look at the previous section.

Assessing personal home pages

All of the generic criteria discussed in Chapter 3 apply in the evaluation of personal home pages. However, there are certain issues which require additional attention. Users often access personal home pages because they want the e-mail address or other contact information for an individual. Thus, this should be available and easy to locate within the site. As mentioned in Chapter 1, personal home pages can be problematic because they often contain little more than images of "These are my friends," "This is my cat," and "This is where I live." Therefore it is of particular concern when evaluating personal home pages to ascertain whether the site provides access to any "real" information. Where information is available, evaluators should assess the coverage and level of detail, as well as the likely value and usefulness of the content. The knowledge and expertise of the author might also be considered, along with the likely accuracy of the information.

CHECKLIST

Assessing organizational WWW sites

☑ What is the purpose of the site?

☑ Are contact details and basic factual information about the institution or organization readily available? Is it easy to locate contact information within the site?

☑ What is the coverage of the site? Does the site simply provide information about the organization, or are additional materials provided?

☑ What is the reputation and expertise of the institution responsible for the information?

☑ What is the likely accuracy of the information?

☑ Is the information current, and is the site well-maintained? Is there an update date for each page of information, or is it otherwise possible to ascertain its currency?

☑ Is the site easily accessible?

☑ Is the information well-presented and arranged?

☑ Is the site easy to use, and are there any user support facilities?

☑ How does the site compare with other similar organizational sites?

☑ What overall impression of the quality of the site is created after examining it?

The tilde

The address or URL of one personal home page mentioned in Chapter 1 is: **http://www.aber.ac.uk/~ddl97/friends/**. The tilde character "~" within this address denotes a student's personal home page at the University of Wales, Aberystwyth. The tilde is often used within the address of WWW sites and pages to denote a personal page within a larger organizational site. However, users should not assume that this is always the case or that the information will be of little value and usefulness. For example, *CyberStacks*, one of the virtual libraries referred to in Chapter 2, contains a tilde in its address, but the site is not a personal home page and is likely to be of value to many users. Conversely, the example discussed below is a personal home page which supplies potentially useful information, but the address does not contain a tilde.

EXAMPLE

Evaluating Phil Bradley's personal home page

Figure 4.2 displays the opening screen to Phil Bradley's home page (**http://www.philb.com**). This example illustrates how home pages can contain potentially useful and valuable information which is likely to be of widespread appeal.

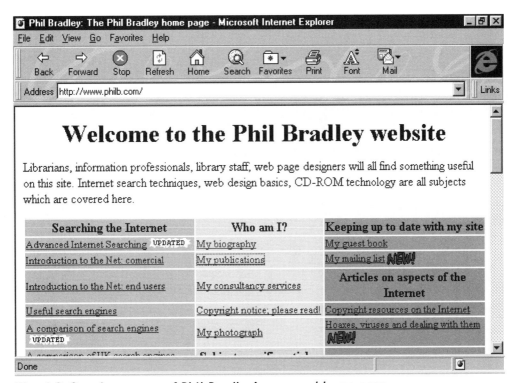

Fig. 4.2 *Opening screen of Phil Bradley's personal home page*

The opening screen (Figure 4.2) immediately tells the user who the site is aimed at: "librarians, information professionals, library staff, web page designers will find something useful on this site." There is also a statement of the intended coverage of the site: "Internet search techniques, web design basics, CD-ROM technology are all subjects which are covered here." Despite its garish colors (the background of the opening screen is yellow and the boxes are in shades of blue, green, orange, magenta, etc.), the page is clearly laid out, and it is immediately obvious what is available and where materials are located. Furthermore, browsing the links from the opening screen to the various documents which are available enables evaluators to build a picture of the potential value of the materials to the intended audience of the site.

Personal information is available about the site author under "my biography," but as can be seen in Figure 4.2, this is not the main focus of the site. The biography serves to underline the knowledge and expertise of Phil Bradley, as his various jobs are listed. Likewise, the list of publications further highlights his authority in the field, as he has written a number of books for three professional library organizations in the UK. Contact details are also available towards the bottom of the opening screen (not visible in Figure 4.2), and there is a counter which suggests the popularity of the site. This site deals with a rapidly changing subject area, and therefore it is important that the information is up-to-date, or that the user is able to ascertain when it was last updated – the author has supplied an update date for most pages, indicating the currency of the information and that the site is well-maintained.

Thus an overall impression of this site is that it not only provides personal and contact information, but is also a source of potentially useful information to library professionals interested in issues relating to accessing and using Internet-based information sources, and that it has been written by a knowledgeable individual who has published in the field.

Subject-based WWW sites

"Subject-based WWW sites" are a collection of pages which have a particular subject focus. As already mentioned in relation to organizational WWW sites and personal home pages, there will be some overlap between these different source types – personal home pages and organizational sites often include materials relating to a specific subject area. Individual pages should be evaluated according to their focus and intended use.

Assessing subject-based WWW sites

The general criteria discussed in Chapter 3 apply in the assessment of subject-based WWW sites. Areas of particular concern are the subject area and types of materials covered, the comprehensiveness of coverage of a site within a specific area, and whether there are any pointers to further information which might

CHECKLIST

Assessing personal home pages

☑ What is the purpose of the site?

☑ What is the coverage of the site? Does the site simply provide links to information of interest to the author, or are materials included which are likely to have a wider appeal?

☑ What is the reputation and expertise of the individual responsible for the information?

☑ Are contact details for the individual concerned readily available? Is it easy to locate contact information within the site?

☑ What is the likely accuracy of the information?

☑ Is the information current and is the site well-maintained? Is there an update date for each page of information, or is it otherwise possible to ascertain its currency?

☑ Is the site easily accessible?

☑ Is the information well-presented and arranged?

☑ Is the site easy to use, and are there any user support facilities?

☑ How does the site compare to other similar sites?

☑ What overall impression of the quality of the site is created after examining it?

enhance the coverage of a source. Some sites are designed as "link sites" (they simply provide hypertext links to relevant materials without contributing any original content), while others offer detailed information on particular subjects. Where sites only link to other resources, the value and usefulness of the links should be considered, including the materials covered, whether they have been selected and on what basis, and whether descriptive information is provided about the various links to provide users with a means to assess their potential usefulness.

The knowledge and expertise of those involved in creating and maintaining a site can affect its overall value and usefulness, as well as the authority and likely accuracy of any information. Therefore, users should consider issues relating to authority, reputation, and expertise. Useful indicators also include whether there are any references to published information and whether there is any sponsorship for the site. Counters can also be used to indicate the popularity of sites, and reviews may be available of sites which are considered particularly valuable within a given subject area. The presentation and arrangement of the source is also of concern as this can make it easier or harder to find information within a site. Evaluators should assess whether a source is clearly, consistently, and logically presented and arranged, and the availability and effectiveness of any features such as a site map, an index, or a search facility to assist in finding information.

EXAMPLE

Evaluating the Vincent van Gogh Information Gallery

Artists and paintings have been an area of interest for many authors of WWW sites and pages, but the resources vary widely in their quality. A search on *Excite* for "Van Gogh" results in 786,783 hits. The first site is "the selected letters of Vincent van Gogh to his brother Theo," and the second, "Van Gogh as comic figure." No further information is provided about the second site (other than the URL), and the curious title makes it sound interesting. However, following the link (**http://www.amherst.edu/~makligma/vgogh.html**) leads to a list of jokes based on the artist's name, rather than to a site about the artist. A user looking for information about Van Gogh is unlikely to be interested in such a page.

Further down the search results is another site, the *Vincent van Gogh Information Gallery* (**http://www.vangoghgallery.com/**). The first page of the site provides a statement indicating its purpose and coverage – the site is described as "the most thorough and comprehensive Van Gogh resource" on the WWW, and claims to include "more than 2,300 pages and 2,315 graphics." In addition, "the site . . . contains information about *all* of Van Gogh's paintings," and includes other related materials.

Coverage

Figure 4.3 displays part of the opening screen to the *Vincent van Gogh Information Gallery*, and exploring some of these links enables the user to build up an impression of the actual coverage of the site.

The "overview" is an account of different stages of Van Gogh's life interspersed with appropriate images (thumbnail images have been used and the

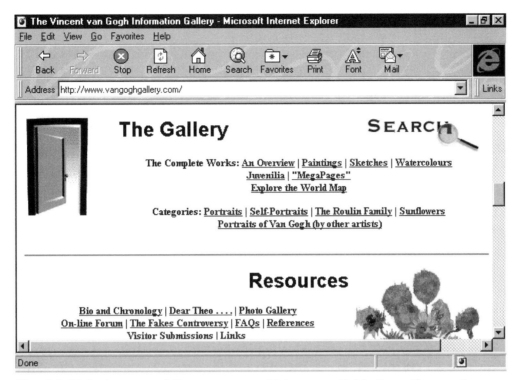

Fig. 4.3 *Links to some of the resources which are available from the opening page of the Vincent van Gogh Information Gallery*

page downloads fairly quickly). "Explore the World Map" is a clickable world map – selecting any of the highlighted sections of the map leads to locations across the world which hold Van Gogh's paintings. The "resources" include a detailed biography and chronology of the artist's life and some of the letters to his brother Theo. The "links" are to a wide range of other networked resources, such as other "Van Gogh specific" sites, "interpretations of Van Gogh's works," and art sites and schools with Van Gogh materials. These add to the coverage of the site, they have been usefully organized, and descriptive and informative details are provided about the links.

Presentation and arrangement

As shown in Figure 4.3, the page is clearly presented, and materials have been usefully organized to enable the user to navigate the site easily. The hypertext links are meaningful, which further facilitates the process of finding resources, and the different pages throughout the site are presented in a familiar format, with the title of the site at the top of each page, which helps users to find their way around. Furthermore, the author includes updating information and an e-mail address.

Authority and reputation

A general impression of this site is that it is an invaluable resource for Van Gogh materials. It is comprehensive in its coverage and it is well-organized and clearly presented. However, there is one drawback. At the end of the first page are various links to "personal" information about the author, David Brooks. He explicitly states that he has a personal interest in the artist rather than any expertise about art or Van Gogh. Thus, readers might be reluctant to rely upon the information. However, there are other indicators of the authority of the site, including extensive facts relating to the origins of the author's interest in the artist, and the site also has sponsorship from a commercial company which produces fine arts and prints. There is a link to "accolades," a collection of badges which the site has been awarded from services such as *Lycos Top 5%* and the *Britannica Internet Guide* (both discussed in Chapter 2). Moreover, the first page includes a counter – there were 577,145 hits since September 1998 (in April 1999), indicating the site's popularity as well as its length of establishment.

Where evaluators are faced with a contradictory situation such as this it can be useful to seek further guidance. *ADAM* (**http://www.adam.ac.uk/**), "the gateway to art, design, architecture, and media information on the Internet," is one of the *eLib* subject-based gateway services discussed in Chapter 2. The service provides access to the descriptions of high-quality materials which have been selected and evaluated by librarians and/or subject experts. A search on *ADAM* for "Van Gogh" results in one hit, the *Vincent van Gogh Information Gallery*. The site is described as "a comprehensive site that aims to cover all Van Gogh's paintings," and details are included of its coverage and features. Therefore, by examining a database of high-quality materials within the appropriate subject area, the reader is provided with confirmation of the quality of this site and an indication of its reputation.

Uniqueness

The lack of other relevant sites listed in *ADAM* also suggests that this is a unique resource for Van Gogh information, and sifting through more of the search results in *Excite* confirms this – no other sites are listed in the first ten hits which sound as if they provide access to the same type of information. Other sites include "Van Gogh Family Tree" (**http://desire.emails.net/lists/jokes/jokes.9807/0046.html**) – more jokes on the artist's name, and "Van Gogh's Ear," the official home page of a "four piece guitar driven band" (**http://members.aol.com/Ndi5idual/index.html**).

CHECKLIST

Assessing subject-based WWW sites

☑ What is the purpose of the site?

☑ What is the coverage of the site? Does the site cover a particular area comprehensively? What subject areas and materials are covered? Are there any pointers to further information and do they enhance the coverage of the site?

☑ Is the site a link site, or does it have any original content? If the site only links to other materials, are the links valuable and useful? What materials are covered by the links? Is descriptive information provided about the links? Does the descriptive information provide users with the means to assess their usefulness?

☑ What is the reputation and expertise of the individual(s) responsible for the site? is the author an expert in the area?

☑ Is there any sponsorship for the site? Does the sponsorship suggest a good reputation?

☑ Is there a counter for the site? Does it indicate that it is popular?

☑ Are there any reviews for the site? Has the site been awarded any badges by rating and reviewing services? Is the site included in any databases of high-quality materials?

☑ What is the likely accuracy of the information? Are there any references to published information?

☑ Is the information current, and is the site well-maintained? Is there an update date for each page of information, or is it otherwise possible to ascertain its currency?

☑ Is the site easily accessible?

☑ Is the information clearly, consistently, and logically presented and arranged? Are there any features such as a site map, an index, or a search facility? How effective are they in assisting users to find information?

☑ Is the site easy to use, and are there any user support facilities?

☑ How does the site compare with other similar sites? Is the site unique in its coverage of the subject area concerned?

☑ What overall impression of the quality of the site is created after examining it?

Electronic journals and magazines

This section covers the evaluation of electronic journals and magazines. It is equally applicable to any other periodical publications such as newspapers or annual reviews. Such publications are often an electronic version of a paper-based equivalent, although an increasing number of journals and magazines are now produced only in an electronic format. It may be appropriate to evaluate the whole publication, or individual articles within it. The level of evaluation will depend upon the needs of the user, and evaluators should select the appropriate criteria from those described below.

Assessing electronic journals and magazines

Electronic journals and electronic journal articles, or magazines and magazine articles, are often accessed on the Internet because they are not otherwise available or because it is more convenient or cheaper. Consequently, they are used and evaluated in much the same way as the printed versions, and many of the criteria are not specific to publications available on the Internet.

Purpose and coverage

The subject area covered is often the chief reason for using such publications, and many of the criteria already described in Chapter 3 in relation to identifying the purpose of a source and assessing its coverage are applicable. Further issues include whether the whole publication is available via the Internet, and if only parts are available, how those parts have been selected. For example, some sites are simply used to advertise a journal or magazine, and therefore offer limited coverage (e.g., the current issue, the contents pages, or selected abstracts). A further factor is whether an archive is available which enables users to access back-dated issues of a publication, and the retrospective coverage of the archive.

Authority and reputation

The general factors affecting the authority and reputation of any source are applicable. However, the reputation and authority of academic journals are complex issues which require further attention. Within a given discipline there is a hierarchy of academic journals which is based upon a combination of factors, including the reputation of the journal, its length of establishment and its impact factor (a measure of the number of times a journal has been cited over a given period divided by the number of articles published in it). The position of a journal within the hierarchy influences perceptions of the quality of the articles published in it, and the result is cyclical: the higher the position of a journal in the hierarchy, the greater the number of articles submitted to it, the more stringent the refereeing process, and thus the higher the quality of the published material. Issues for evaluation include whether the journal is refereed, the stringency of the refereeing process (this might be determined by examining rejection rates for the journal), its reputation and impact factor, and its genealogy (the length of establishment and whether there is a printed equivalent for the journals). Methods of assessing reputation include determining whether a journal is covered by any bibliographical databases, such as MEDLINE for medical journals or *ERIC* for education journals. Further aspects are the reputation and experience of the editorial board and the reputation and experience of any sponsors or other organizations involved in the production of the publication. Some of these issues would obviously also be applicable to nonacademic publications.

However, the reputation of a journal is not always a useful indicator of quality. For example, a highly reputable journal such as *The Lancet* is not of interest to every medical professional because of its broad subject coverage. Therefore, the subject area and the needs of the user remain central to the evaluation process. Moreover, a newly established electronic journal, with no paper-based equivalent, may have a reputable editorial board and the support of a reputable learned society (sponsorship by a learned society indicates an academic need rather than a commercial opportunity), and there may be demand for the journal in its particular subject area. The various criteria cannot be used independently, and while authority and reputation are important, they should be considered in relation to factors such as coverage, currency, and accuracy.

Accuracy

The general factors discussed in Chapter 3 relating to assessing accuracy are applicable in the evaluation of individual journal or magazine articles. However, determining the accuracy of academic articles may be problematic, because the quality of the research is a central consideration and the evaluator may not have the necessary expertise to assess this. Therefore, readers might need to consider the wider range of issues discussed in Chapter 3 which affect accuracy and how it is perceived. In addition, the refereeing and editing of academic journals (discussed above) are considered essential quality filters which increase confidence in the accuracy and reliability of information published in a journal.

Currency and maintenance

The general factors relating to currency and maintenance are also applicable. Additional factors are the length of time between acceptance of an article by a journal and its subsequent publication, as well as whether there is any time difference between the publication of the printed and electronic versions of the same issue. Evaluators may need to average these figures over several past issues. In addition, due to the nature of electronic information, it may be possible to revise and update articles. If an article has been revised, the details should be clearly visible.

Further issues

The general factors relating to the accessibility of journals and their presentation and arrangement are applicable, but there are some additional considerations. Cost is a central concern, and evaluators should consider the charging options available, as well as the availability of any free information. Where an archive is available, there should be a search facility which is accessible by subject, author, volume, and issue number, and it should be possible to limit searches by date range. An index for the site as a whole will be useful, and it should be easy to locate the latest copy of a journal or magazine, as well as any back issues. A contents list should be available for each issue, and there should be links between the citations at the end of articles and the main body of the text. Additional features which take advantage of the electronic format include the ability to update articles, to e-mail comments on articles, and to link directly into other electronic resources. Where such facilities are available, they should be appraised according to whether they add value to the publication.

As discussed in Chapter 3 under assessing accessibility, some sites use PDF to display materials in a high-quality format. PDF is often used to display journal or magazine articles as they would appear in a paper-based publication, and evaluators may need to consider whether this option is available, as well as whether it is easy to download the necessary software and to access the article concerned.

The comparison issues are also applicable. In particular, evaluators might consider the advantages of the electronic format over the paper-based equivalent, the relative currency of an electronic version compared with the printed version, including the frequency of updating, and the relative coverage of the two versions.

EXAMPLE

Evaluating Ariadne

Ariadne (**http://www.ariadne.ac.uk/**) is an electronic journal produced as part of the *eLib* program, which is aimed at librarians and other information professionals. The opening screen provides a statement of the intended audience (subject librarians and other librarians working in academic libraries) and the aims of the site (to describe and evaluate sources and services available via the Internet of potential use to librarians and information professionals, and to report on the progress of *eLib*). The statement also includes the format (printed and electronic), the frequency of updating (every other month), the differing coverage of the two formats (all of the printed contents are available via the WWW, as well as some additional materials), and that the journal is freely distributed to every academic library and computer center within the UK. In addition, the two formats are produced simultaneously and the WWW version is sometimes updated in between issues with news or events. Therefore, within the first page, the user is provided with thorough details of the intended purpose and coverage of the journal. However, evaluators would also need to examine the site to ascertain more about the publication and whether it meets these aims and objectives.

A link on the opening screen leads to the current issue of the journal and browsing this gives a clearer picture of its contents. For example, the contents page is divided into editorials, main articles, updates on *eLib*, regular columns, and reports on events. There is a link to each article, details of the author(s), a sentence describing each article, and a tag indicating whether each article appears on the WWW only or both on the WWW and in print. Browsing the contents page of the current issue indicates that the journal is indeed of interest to librarians and information professionals interested in the Internet and networked information sources, and selecting any of the links leads directly to the full articles. It is also possible to access past issues of the journal – following the link from the opening screen to "further details of back issues" results in Figure

4.4. This page displays a brief summary of the contents of each issue with a link to the full issue.

Presentation and arrangement

The whole of the *Ariadne* site is clearly and logically arranged. The presentation format displayed in Figure 4.4 is consistent throughout the site – the journal title is displayed at the top of each screen with an indication of where the user is within the site (here it is "back issues of Ariadne"), and various options or shortcuts are displayed on each page. A link to the current issue of the journal is clearly displayed on the opening screen, and there are also links to the back issues. From each article, it is possible to move back to the contents list of the current journal or to the opening page of the site. It is also possible to search the whole site, including the back issues; the search facility is easy to use, and help information is provided.

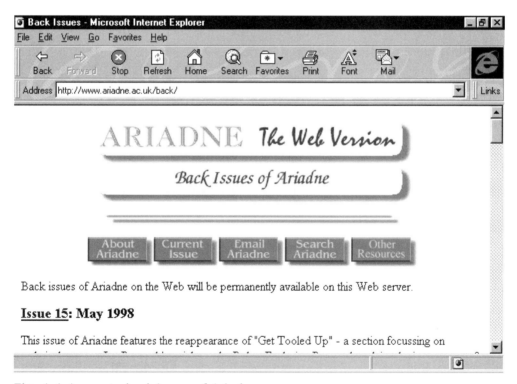

Fig. 4.4 *Access to back issues of Ariadne*

Authority and reputation

The journal is not refereed, but it is possible to determine its authority as details of the project team and editorial board are given. These are all individuals working in the library or information science professions. Moreover, sponsorship details are included on the first page – as already noted, *Ariadne* is part of the *eLib* project and it is sponsored by the Joint Information Systems Committee, a centrally funded national committee within the UK.

Cost of electronic journals and magazines

This example has illustrated some of the techniques which might be used to evaluate an electronic journal. However, one factor which has not been discussed is the cost and any restrictions to access. In this case, *Ariadne* is freely available via the WWW and there are no restrictions on accessing the journal. The example of *The Lancet* was used in Chapter 3 to illustrate evaluating the cost and value for money of a resource – *The Lancet* is available as an electronic version of the printed publication, but to access the site, users must register, and to access the whole publication, users must subscribe to the journal. Therefore, readers are recommended to refer back to the section on accessibility in Chapter 3 for further information on these aspects of evaluation.

CHECKLIST

Assessing electronic journals and magazines

☑ What is the purpose of the site? What are the aims and objectives of the site providing access to the journal or magazine? Is the site intended simply for advertising purposes?

☑ What is the coverage of the site? Is the whole journal or magazine available? If only parts are available, how are those parts selected?

☑ Is there an archive for accessing back issues of the journal or magazine? What is the retrospective coverage of the archive? Is the archive searchable by subject, author, issue, and/or volume number? Is it possible to limit searches by date range? How useful and effective is the search facility?

☑ What is the reputation of the journal or magazine? Is it an authoritative journal or magazine? What are the reputation and experience of the editorial board? What are the reputation and experience of any other organizations involved in the production of the journal or magazine?

☑ In relation to academic journals: What is the reputation of the journal? What is the impact factor of the journal? What is the genealogy of the journal? How long has it been available? Is there a paper-based equivalent? Is the journal refereed, and how stringent is the refereeing process? Is the journal indexed in any appropriate bibliographical databases?

☑ Is the site well-maintained? Is there a time delay between article acceptance and publication in the journal? What is the time delay? Is there a time difference between production of the printed and electronic publications? Is there a facility for updating articles? Are details provided of any updating procedures?

☑ Is the site easily accessible?

☑ Is the information well-presented and arranged? Is there a site index? How easy is it to locate individual issues within the site? Is there a contents list for each issue? Is it easy to locate individual articles? Are there links between citations and the main body of the text in each article?

☑ Are there any additional features, such as to e-mail comments on articles, or to link directly into other electronic sources? Do these add value to the journal or magazine?

☑ Can articles be displayed in PDF? Is it easy to download the necessary software and access the article concerned?

☑ Is the site easy to use, and are there any user support facilities?

☑ How does the site compare with other similar sites?

☑ What overall impression of the quality of the site is created after examining it?

Image-based and multimedia sources

Image-based information sources are sources which primarily rely upon the use of images as a source of information, whereas multimedia sources rely on a combination of media, such as sound, images, and video clips. The Internet is increasingly being used as a source of graphical and multimedia information, for example to illustrate work, for presentations, to supplement other textual materials, or for computer assisted learning (CAL) materials (multimedia teaching packs which are designed to enhance the learning experience through the use of computing technology). Image-based and multimedia sources may include a large textual component, but the purpose of the criteria in this section is to enable sites to be assessed in terms of their image or other nontextual content. Evaluation may be required for a whole site which provides access to images or other media, or for an individual image which forms part of an otherwise text-based source of information. Evaluators should select the appropriate criteria from those described below, depending upon the circumstances.

Assessing image-based and multimedia sources

In relation to the purpose and coverage of a site or source, evaluation should include the topics covered by individual images, video or sound clips, the range of different subjects covered as a whole, and the comprehensiveness of coverage within an area. For example, a site might contain images of the life cycle of an animal, and considerations would include whether all the major stages have been covered, the number of images for each stage, and whether the depth of coverage is appropriate for the user (a university or college student will require more detail than a high school student). Explanatory text about any images or other media can enhance their value. Factors for assessment include the level of detail, the balance of text and images or other media, and whether the explanatory text is sufficient for the needs of the user. In addition, pointers to further information may enhance the coverage of a site.

The nature of images and other nontextual media as a source of information may mean that their reputation and authority, their accuracy, and their currency are less important. However, a site which adopts a particular perspective may contain biased images, and images may become outdated, in which case a site which is regularly updated will be of more value. Factors for consideration therefore include whether the date is given when each image, video clip, or sound was produced, whether they are regularly updated, and the motivation and expertise of those responsible for producing them. One further concern is the authority of resources which are designed for educational purposes – assessors should consider whether material is provided commercially or by an academic institution, as this can affect perceptions of reliability.

Accessibility

The generic accessibility issues discussed in Chapter 3 are applicable here. Factors specifically relevant to this type of source include:

- the availability of contact and copyright information, as it is frustrating for users to locate an appropriate image or multimedia resource, and then to be unable to identify any copyright information or to contact the person responsible for its production
- the computer file format used, which must be compatible with the software and hardware available to the user
- the speed of accessing materials; the file size of materials will affect access speeds, and sites might usefully provide a local mirror site, or use thumbnail images.

The accessibility of CAL materials is of concern, as students and pupils may have limited network access or access via slow computers. It may be possible to download a self-contained package using FTP for local use, or materials might be accessible only via a WWW site which is likely to be much slower. The mode of access should be evaluated in relation to the speed of access, as well as to the ease of use.

Presentation and arrangement

The presentation and arrangement of a site providing access to nontextual resources will affect ease of access and use, and again the generic criteria apply. A particular issue is the availability of navigational features to assist users in moving between different materials. In addition, evaluators should assess the availability of any features or facilities which take advantage of the multimedia format. For educational materials, examples include tutorials, self-test materials, images, and video graphics. Considerations include the availability of such features, whether they add value to the content, and whether they enhance the learning experience. Further factors are the clarity of images or video clips, whether they are in color or black-and-white, and whether images are two-dimensional or three-dimensional. Information on the size and resolution of the images may be available – the resolution will affect the quality and clarity of the images. However, the quality of materials may be difficult to reconcile with the speed of access, as the higher the quality of the images, video, or sound clips, the longer they will take to download, and the more computer storage space they will require.

Comparison with other sources

An assessment of the value of image-based and multimedia materials will require comparison with others that are available. Evaluators could compare images with those available in books, and assess whether a site offers access to a unique source of materials, or provides access to information in a unique or innovative format through the use of multimedia. For example, CAL materials are used because educators wish to offer materials in an innovative format in order to enhance the learning experience, and a CAL package might offer unique features or facilities.

EXAMPLE

Evaluating Bigcats.com

Figure 4.5 displays part of a page from a collection of images of wild cats (**http://www.bigcats.com/image/index.html**). A teacher might use this site if she or he were interested in finding images of wild cats for a class. In certain

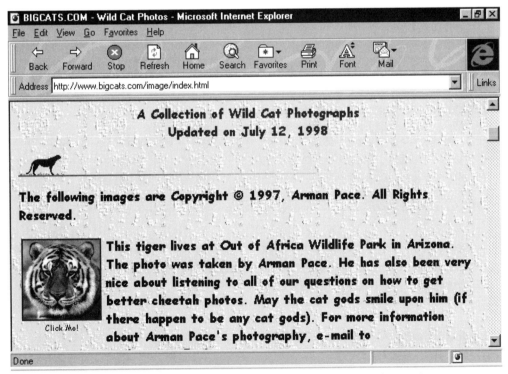

Fig. 4.5 *Collection of wild cat photographs with copyright information*

107

respects, this site would be useful – thumbnail images have been used and the teacher could quite easily and quickly browse through the page shown in Figure 4.5 to identify any images that she or he might want to view in full. The images are clear and in color, copyright information is clearly displayed, and there is some textual information about each image.

However, there are drawbacks to this site. The textual details offer little descriptive information about the images, other than the individual responsible and where the photos were taken. A user would therefore have to consult a separate source for facts about the animals shown. The site is not comprehensive in its coverage of wild cats, but only includes a limited number of images. Other linked parts of the site include video files which are very slow to download, pages about the development of WWW sites, and references to published articles on cheetahs. Therefore, an overall impression of this site would be that it provides access to a limited number of potentially useful images of wild cats, but that the site itself would not be suitable for children to browse independently as they could not simultaneously read about the images or follow useful links to further information.

CHECKLIST

Assessing image-based and multimedia sources

☑ What is the purpose of the site?

☑ What is the coverage of the site? What topics are covered by individual images, video, or sound clips? What is the range of different subjects covered as a whole? is the site comprehensive within an area?

☑ Is explanatory text available? What level of detail is provided in any explanatory text? Is the explanatory text sufficient for the needs of the user? Does the explanatory text enhance the value of the images or other nontextual materials? Is the balance of text and images or other nontextual materials appropriate?

☑ Are there any pointers to further information which enhance the coverage of the site?

☑ What is the reputation of the source? Is it an authoritative source? For teaching materials: Is the material provided commercially or by an academic institution?

☑ Is the information current, and is the site well-maintained? Is there a date of production for any images or other nontextual materials? Are there any details of updating? What is the motivation and expertise of those responsible for maintaining the materials?

☑ Is the site easily accessible?

☑ Is there a mirror site?

☑ Have thumbnail images been used?

☑ Is copyright information available? Are contact details available?

☑ For teaching materials: Is it possible to download a self-contained package using FTP for local use, or are materials accessed via a WWW site? Does the mode of access affect the speed?

☑ Is information available on the file formats? What file formats are used?

☑ Is information available on file sizes? What are the file sizes of materials?

☑ Is the information well-presented and arranged? Is it easy to navigate between different images or materials? Are images or other nontextual materials clear? What is the image resolution?

☑ Are images in color or black-and-white? Are images two-dimensional, three-dimensional, or video clips?

☑ Are there any features or facilities that take advantage of the multimedia format? Do any such features or facilities add value to the content of the site?

☑ Is the site easy to use, and are there any user support facilities?

☑ How does the site compare with other similar sites?

☑ What overall impression of the quality of the site is created after examining it?

Usenet newsgroups and discussion lists

"Discussion lists," also sometimes called "mailing lists" or "listservs," are e-mail based lists available to a group of users who are interested in a particular topic area. Software is used to enable e-mail users to subscribe to a list, and they can then post messages to the whole group, participate in discussions, and receive all the messages which are posted. Usenet newsgroups are a world-wide distributed system of bulletin boards which are arranged hierarchically into topic areas. These are similar to discussion lists in that different users can discuss a particular area of interest, but users do not have to subscribe, and anyone can view the messages provided they have access to the software required. In order to access or post a message to a newsgroup, a newsgroup reader has previously been required, but newsgroups may now also be accessed using a WWW browser.

Usenet newsgroups and discussion lists are therefore differentiated by the means of accessing the information. However, there are similarities in the nature of the information disseminated via the two routes, and consequently there are many similarities in the techniques which might be used to assess the quality of that information. Furthermore, many discussion lists are also accessible via Usenet and vice versa. Both types of sources are therefore discussed together here, although the criteria are differentiated where applicable.

There are three ways in which Usenet newsgroups and discussion lists are commonly used: users may wish to post a query or a reply, they may "lurk" in a newsgroup or list (i.e., read the messages and follow the discussion but without posting a message), or they may want to browse an earlier discussion using an archive. Thus, evaluators may be concerned with assessing an individual message or with evaluating the whole newsgroup or discussion list as an information source, and the appropriate criteria should be selected from those described below.

Assessing Usenet newsgroups and discussion lists

The generic criteria discussed in Chapter 3 relating to identifying the purpose of a source are applicable here. Some newsgroups and discussion lists have a charter or FAQ which might provide useful information about the intended subject coverage and audience. In addition, the intended coverage of a group can often be ascertained from the group's name, or by examining the group's home page where one is available.

The generic criteria relating to coverage are also applicable to either individual messages or whole newsgroups and discussion lists. A particular issue is the type of material (some might be used to post job advertisements or advertisements for new WWW sites, while others will be intended for the discussion of a specific issue). Evaluators could browse recent messages in order to determine whether discussion focuses upon the intended area. Other considerations are whether real exchange and discussion takes place in the group, as indicated by the proportion of questions answered and whether discussion threads develop, or whether the group largely comprises one-off messages. If an individual, usually described as the moderator, is responsible for monitoring or moderating the content of a group, the discussion might be more focused on the intended subject area. It is often possible to determine whether a group is moderated by consulting any introductory information.

Participants

The participants in a group can influence its overall value and usefulness, as well as the topics which are discussed. Usenet newsgroups and discussion lists are useful for contacting a large number of people, for contacting people all over the world or in a particular locality, or for contacting a subset of a population (for example, general medical practitioners in the UK). Therefore, factors requiring examination are the number of people involved, whether the list is local, national, or international, and the actual composition of the group. These criteria are more relevant to discussion lists, where participants subscribe to the list, and where there may be a publicly viewable membership list on the home page. However, where a list of members is unavailable, or in relation to Usenet newsgroups, evaluators could examine recent messages as an indication of the participants. Newsgroups and discussion lists are sometimes used to seek advice or opinions from others. In medicine, examples might include asking others about their experiences with a piece of equipment or their attitudes towards a treatment or drug. A discussion list or newsgroup may have a reputation as a useful source of ideas and opinions, and reviews may be available to indicate this. It may also be necessary to establish the likely knowledge and expertise of the participants, as well as the expertise of an individual author.

Accuracy and authority

The questionable accuracy and authority of information retrieved via Usenet newsgroups and discussion lists is often considered their main drawback. However, users do not necessarily expect to rely upon the information, and essentially newsgroups and discussion lists are used less as a source of high-quality information than as a useful way of contacting people and seeking their advice or opinions. Therefore, some of the general criteria relating to accuracy from Chapter 3 are relevant, such as whether the author of a message is a well-known expert, or whether a refereed journal article is cited in a message.

However, evaluators should bear in mind the informal nature of the information and the purpose for which it will be used.

Hernández-Borges, et al. have developed a methodology for analyzing the likely authority of various paediatrics mailing lists.[1] MEDLINE was searched for the names of list subscribers, and an impact factor was calculated for each of the subscribers using the *Science Citation Index*. An average impact factor was calculated for each list, as well as an average impact factor per participant and per message to the group. An average number of postings per participant over a given time period was also calculated. The authors claim that their methodology offers a technique for assessing the quality of mailing lists because it is "based on the accumulation of defined impact factors generated by published articles of the various members of the discussion groups, a way for any scientific group to gain prestige in a given field of science." However, while this technique sounds worthwhile, the process is perhaps too complex for many evaluators seriously to consider.

Accessibility and volume of traffic

The accessibility issues discussed in Chapter 3 are not generally applicable here. Those issues which do require consideration are whether there are any restrictions to access (some discussion lists have a closed membership), and the mode of access (whether a discussion list or Usenet newsgroup).

A further concern is the likely volume of traffic to a group, which can sometimes be unmanageably large. In order to monitor the volume, evaluators could browse a newsgroup, examine the archive where available, or subscribe to a discussion list for a limited time-period. One author has proposed a technique which involves calculating the average number of messages per day and categorizing the messages according to whether they are administrative, announcements, discussion, pointers to further information, etc.[2] The group characteristics can then be profiled according to the volume of postings and the nature of the messages, such as "very light traffic consisting entirely of announcements" or an "active forum . . . dominated by relevant discussion." A useful facility is the ability to receive messages in a digest of the day's or week's postings as one message. The frequency of such a digest might need to be considered.

The availability of an archive will affect the usefulness of a newsgroup or discussion list as an information source, and the retrospective coverage of the archive is a consideration (some archives are maintained for as little as a month). The availability of facilities for searching the archive will affect its accessibility, and it is useful if the archive is browsable by date, author, and subject thread. A searchable archive may be available from a home page, or text files of discussion threads might be downloadable from an FTP site.

Ease of use

The issues relating to presentation and arrangement, ease of use, and user support are generally irrelevant here. One factor to be considered is whether the group has adopted conventions for labeling messages according to whether they provide information about jobs, conferences, etc., as this can facilitate the process of sifting through the volume of postings. Other issues relate to administration. If there is an individual responsible for list administration, any problems which arise, such as mail loops (an individual's e-mail system automatically replies to a group, they receive that reply, the system automatically replies back again, etc.), may be dealt with more quickly. Likewise, administrative and help information may be available via a home page or might be posted regularly to the group. Such information should cover, not only the intended coverage and audience as mentioned, but also how to subscribe, unsubscribe, and post messages to the group. The usefulness of any such information will obviously need to be assessed.

EXAMPLE

Evaluating the Postmodern-Christian discussion list

The *Postmodern-Christian* list is a UK-based discussion list provided by the *Mailbase* service. *Mailbase* is a service which runs thousands of discussion lists and provides details of all of them on the WWW (**http://www.mailbase.ac.uk**). This site is a useful source on the intended purpose, coverage, and participants of different lists, and other discussion list providers elsewhere in the world also offer similar services. Thus, it is often useful to search for a discussion list or Usenet newsgroup using a search engine to determine whether any such information is available.

Figure 4.6 displays the information provided on the *Mailbase* site about the *Postmodern-Christian* discussion list (**http://www.mailbase.ac.uk/lists/postmodern-christian/**). The opening paragraph indicates the intended participants and coverage of the group: "Researchers and practitioners . . . exploring cultural and theological issues raised by postmodern society and Christian faith." The opening screen includes links to further list information, a membership list, the owners of the list, files added by the list owners, the archives, a search facility

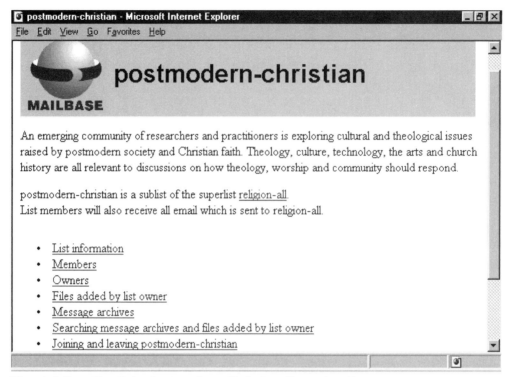

Fig. 4.6 *Details of the Postmodern-Christian discussion list*

for the archives, and information on joining and leaving the list. Individuals interested in evaluating the likely usefulness of the *Postmodern-Christian* list can therefore browse these links in order to make an assessment.

The list information includes the number of members (142), the subject category (humanities), when the list started (October 1994), the last posting to the list (the same day as the page was accessed), the total number of messages (9,271), and the average number of messages per month (201). This indicates a well-established group with a fairly small membership but a fairly high volume of traffic. Further details include statements that access to the list is unrestricted, it is not moderated, anyone can send and receive messages, and there is an archive which is freely accessible. Browsing the membership list indicates that the group is of worldwide appeal and that it is by no means restricted to users within academia. The files added by the list owner are a further source of useful information, and in particular, the first is "approach2scripture" which is provided because "list discussion often grinds to a halt because of conflicting views." The file is "a quick summary of the main views," and therefore a useful indicator of the discussions which the list focuses upon.

Coverage

The only effective method of assessing the likely value of a Usenet newsgroup or discussion list will be either to follow the discussion or to browse the archive. *Mailbase* allows users to search the archives of its lists or to browse messages by date, thread, subject, or author. Browsing the messages by thread results in a clear display of the topics which have been discussed during the past two years, and the number of people who have posted on each topic and who they are; it is also possible to view the messages. For example, a recent topic at the time of writing was "God(s) and the world cup." Numerous people posted messages in relation to this discussion, indicating that this list does not consist of one-off messages, but involves real discussion of topical issues. Examining any of the individual messages suggests the discussion is informal and not of an academic nature, which is suggested both by the group's name and the description provided on the opening page of the list's site. Therefore, the list is likely to be of interest to a wide audience interested in topical issues which might have an impact upon Christianity.

CHECKLIST

Assessing Usenet newsgroups and discussion lists

☑ What is the purpose of the discussion list or newsgroup? Is there a home page or FAQ?

☑ What is the coverage of the discussion list or newsgroup?

☑ Does real exchange and discussion take place via the discussion list or newsgroup, or does it largely consist of one-off messages?

☑ Is the discussion list or newsgroup moderated?

☑ What is the reputation of the discussion list or newsgroup?

☑ Is there a list of group members or participants? Who are the participants in the group? How many participants are there? Is the group local, national, or international? What is the likely knowledge and expertise of the participants? Are there any restrictions to accessing or subscribing to the group? Does the group have a closed membership?

☑ For individual messages: What is the likely accuracy of the information? What is the reputation and expertise of the author? What is the date of the message? Is an original source of information cited in the message?

☑ What is the average volume of traffic? Is the volume manageable?

☑ Is it possible to receive messages in a digest? How frequently is the digest distributed?

☑ Has the group adopted conventions for labeling messages?

☑ Is an archive available? Are files of discussion threads downloadable from an FTP site? What is the retrospective coverage of the archive? Is there a facility for searching the archive? Is the archive browsable by date, author, and subject thread? Is help information available for searching the archive?

☑ Is an individual responsible for the group administration? Is any administrative or help information available? Is the information periodically posted to the group? How useful is the information? Is the intended coverage and audience of the group described? Are details of how to subscribe, unsubscribe, and post messages included?

☑ How does the discussion list or newsgroup compare with others?

☑ What overall impression of the quality of the discussion list or newsgroup is created after examining it?

Databases

"Databases" are a collection of records each of which contains details of a different data item, whether numeric, textual, or image-based, and which are usually available in a searchable format. There are a wide range of sources available via the Internet which might be described as databases, including library catalogs, commercial catalogs, and bibliographical databases. Some databases were previously available electronically or as a printed index, while others have been developed specifically for use via the WWW or Telnet. Many of the criteria therefore refer to databases generally, while others are peculiar to accessing databases via the Internet.

Assessing databases

Readers should begin by examining any introductory information or help files, as this is often a useful source of information on the intended purpose, coverage, and audience of a database. Evaluators will also need to consider the subject areas and types of materials covered, the retrospective coverage, and the comprehensiveness of the database. A number of searches could be conducted on the database in order to assess its coverage and whether the aims and objectives have been achieved. When reviewing bibliographical databases in particular, comprehensiveness might be assessed by determining the number of journals or other materials indexed within a particular subject area. In addition, the coverage of a database will be enhanced by links to any other electronic sources, such as to the full-text of articles in a bibliographical database.

Level of detail in database records

An important factor to be considered is the level of detail provided in each record of the database and the value and usefulness of that information. For example, bibliographical databases are used via the Internet to search for references to published information. If users can make an informed assessment of the relevance of a publication from the information provided by a database, then that database will be of more value. Database providers may stipulate the level of detail, or the evaluator could examine a sample of the records in order to make an assessment. A further issue in relation to bibliographical databases is whether abstracts have been truncated by word length, as this can be frustrating where valuable information has been omitted. Furthermore, evaluators may wish to consider the expertise of the authors involved in producing database records as an indication of their likely usefulness – if journal article abstracts are written by their original authors then it can be assumed that the abstracts will provide an accurate indication of the articles' content.

Reputation

Evaluators should consider the reputation of a database and the authority of any institutions concerned with its production. Some databases are well-known and heavily used within a particular subject area because they are valuable. Similarly a new database might be produced by a well-known organization with extensive experience in database production, indicating its likely value and usefulness. A guide to reference works, such as *Walford's*, could also be examined, as inclusion of a database in such a guide provides an indication of its reputation.

Accuracy

Many of the general accuracy issues discussed in Chapter 3 are not applicable. However, citation accuracy is essential in bibliographical databases, as wrong page numbers or journal volumes will result in wasted time for the user. Likewise, any typographical or spelling errors can render any database less useful. Evaluators could examine a number of references to estimate their accuracy, or where possible they could examine the index for commonly misspelled terms (when examining the index to a database, records can be displayed as, for example, an alphabetical list of author names or journal titles – it is much easier to spot spelling mistakes when records are displayed in this way).

Currency and maintenance

Currency and maintenance are central considerations in the assessment of any database, as they are commonly used to access the latest information about a topic or issue. In order to judge currency, it may be possible to ascertain how frequently the database is updated from any introductory information or by searching the database for recent additions. Another factor is the time delay between the publication of materials and their appearance in a bibliographical database. Again, it may be possible to determine this from any introductory information or by searching for recent publications.

Presentation, arrangement, and search facilities

The presentation and arrangement of a database will affect the ease with which a user can access the information it contains. In addition to the general factors discussed in Chapter 3, evaluators should consider the searching and browsing facilities which are available. The particular facilities which are available will be dependent upon the individual source, but they should enable users to retrieve information quickly and easily, and different modes of access should be available for accessing the same data. In relation to bibliographical databases, certain basic features should be available, including the ability to search by author, title, or subject keyword, as well as the ability to limit by publication type and date range. Some databases offer more sophisticated searching facilities, such as automatic keyword mapping and the ability to amend and rerun search statements in MEDLINE, and the citation search option in the BIDS ISI databases.

Any available search or browse facilities should be assessed in terms of their effectiveness, their ease of use, and their value. They should also be evaluated according to whether they meet the needs of the intended user group. Further points relate to the ease of outputting and downloading data from the database, including the ability to export data into another package. For example, academic users might maintain a personal database of bibliographical references, and it is therefore useful if references can be transferred into a reference management package or a word processor without the need for data conversion. In addition, some databases offer facilities to output results via e-mail, and the available output options should be examined. Furthermore, some databases are in the form of a catalog where material is available for loan or purchase. Under such circumstances, it should be possible to order material directly via the source, and contact information should be readily available.

Further issues

Again, the generic issues discussed in Chapter 3 under accessibility are of relevance here, particularly the speed and reliability of access, and whether there are any restrictions, such as a charge to access a database or to download records. Likewise, the issues relating to ease of use and user support are applicable, and the availability of help information is of particular concern. Evaluators would need to use a database to determine whether it is intuitive and user-friendly, and examine any help information to assess its usefulness. Many databases are unique in their coverage, and this should be a consideration during assessment. In addition, during recent years, various versions of MEDLINE have been made freely available on the Internet, and relevant considerations include the difference between the coverage of any free versions of a database and that of the original,[3] and comparisons of the coverage of the same data by different databases.

EXAMPLE

Evaluating PubMed

As mentioned above, during recent years various versions of MEDLINE have been made available via the Internet, and PubMed is one of these. The opening screen to PubMed (**http://www.ncbi.nlm.nih.gov/PubMed/**) is displayed in Figure 4.7. As can be seen, there is a statement of the intended coverage of the database – access to the 9 million citations held in the original MEDLINE database plus pre-MEDLINE (basic data which has not yet been added to MEDLINE, indicating the currency of the source). The site also provides access to other related databases, including some molecular biology resources. The authority of MEDLINE as a database for healthcare and medical resources is

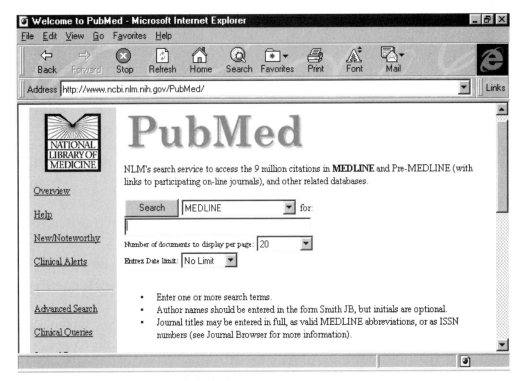

Fig. 4.7 *Opening screen of PubMed*

almost unquestionable – it is produced by the National Library of Medicine at the US National Institute for Health, and is the most widely used bibliographical database in the field. This version of the database claims to cover the whole of MEDLINE and it is also provided by the National Library of Medicine.

Search facilities

The search input box is shown in Figure 4.7 – this is described as the simple search interface and an option is also displayed for advanced searching. As can be seen, users can enter one or more search terms, including author names, subject terms, or journal titles. The advanced search option enables users to specify which field or fields of the database they wish to search (for example, the author field or article title field), to specify a search mode and to combine terms using "and," "or," and "not."

There are many more options for searching MEDLINE via the PubMed site. For example, users can browse the subject headings used to index materials in the database and add these to their search, and they can modify and rerun search statements. Another notable example is the "clinical queries using research methodology filters" – this enables users to search the database only for materials with a research basis, an invaluable feature for clinicians and other healthcare professionals. There is also a journal browser which would enable an evaluator to determine whether the journals they are interested in are covered by the database.

Searching PubMed to assess coverage

Conducting a fairly straightforward search on PubMed indicates some of the features further, as well as the coverage of the database. A search for "breast" and "cancer" retrieves 88,952 documents. Users can specify how many documents they want to view, or they can opt to modify their search by specifying a date limit, adding new terms, or restricting their search to certain fields within the database. Related terms used to index materials within the database are also displayed and these can be used to modify a search – in this example "neoplasms" and "carcinoma" are given as alternatives to the broader term "cancer." Selecting to display the first twenty hits of the search leads to a list of the titles, authors, and journal details, and users can then select the relevant articles to download or view. The full display of any references includes a detailed and informative abstract which generally provides sufficient information for users to assess the relevance of any materials and whether they wish to order the full article (this can be done directly from PubMed).

All of the options discussed above are easy to use. Brief, context-sensitive help information is continuously displayed throughout the system, including the different options available – for example, in Figure 4.7 the search options are listed underneath the query input box. This information is clear and understandable. There are also links to more detailed help information throughout the site, and again this is easy to use and understand. There is an option to send questions and comments to a "help desk" (evaluators would need to use this in order to assess the response times and the usefulness of any responses). Help information and the availability of user support were also discussed in Chapter 3 in relation to the *BIDS ISI* database and readers are recommended to examine this section for further details.

Further issues

The above discussion has illustrated the application of some of the criteria which might be used in the evaluation of a database which is available via the Internet. As indicated in the earlier section on "assessing databases," there are a number of issues which have not yet been mentioned. An evaluator would need to consider the accessibility of a database – there are currently no restrictions to accessing PubMed, and the database is freely available to anyone with an

Internet connection. However, this is not always the case, and evaluators would need to consider the costs involved and the value of accessing a database via the Internet in comparison with any other options which might be available. Those interested in using this database regularly might also need to compare it with others that are available, and to consider their overall impression of the quality of the site. From the inspection discussed here, the comprehensiveness of coverage of the site is evident, as it includes the whole of the MEDLINE database, as well as access to other related databases, and there are a wide range of invaluable features for searching and retrieving the information.

CHECKLIST

Assessing databases

☑ What is the intended purpose, coverage, and audience of the database? Is this information available from any introductory information or help files?

☑ What is the coverage of the database? What subject areas and materials are covered? Is the database comprehensive within a particular area? What is the retrospective coverage of the database? Is information available regarding the material which is included in the database? Are there links to further sources of information?

☑ Are different versions of the same database available? Are there any differences in coverage?

☑ How much information is provided in each record of the database? Is the amount of information useful? Is the amount of information sufficient for the needs of the user?

☑ For bibliographical databases: Do they consist of references only, or are abstracts available? For what percentage of the database are abstracts provided? Have the abstracts been truncated by word length?

☑ Is it possible to identify the authors responsible for the records in the database? What are their knowledge and expertise?

☑ What is the reputation of the database? Is the database included in any guides to reference works, such as *Walford's*?

☑ Are there any typographical or spelling errors? Are there any errors in bibliographical citations? Are there any quality-control procedures?

☑ Is the database current and well-maintained? How frequently is the database updated? Is there a time delay between the publication of materials and their appearance in the database?

☑ Is the information well-presented and arranged? What searching and browsing facilities are available? Are any searching and browsing facilities useful, effective, and easy to use? What outputting and downloading options are available? Is it easy to output and download data from the database? Can data be exported into another package? Is this easy to do?

☑ In relation to bibliographical databases: Is it possible to search by author, title, or subject keyword? Can searches be limited by publication type and date range? Are there any additional searching or browsing features? Are the search and browse facilities effective, easy to use, and useful?

☑ Is it possible to order material directly from the database? Is contact information available?

☑ Is the database easily accessible? Are there any restrictions to access? Is there a charge to access the database or to download records?

☑ Is the database easy to use, and are there any user support facilities?

☑ How does the database compare with other similar databases?

☑ What overall impression of the quality of the database is created after examining it?

FTP archives

FTP stands for File Transfer Protocol, the standard or protocol which enables users to transfer files from one computer to another. An FTP archive is a collection of files of software, textual materials or numerical data, which can be accessed and retrieved using FTP. FTP archives were previously only accessible using an FTP utility. However, it is now possible to access them using a WWW browser such as *Netscape Navigator* or *Internet Explorer*, and some sites are now also designed for use via the WWW.

The issues discussed in this section relate to an evaluation of the sites themselves rather than an evaluation of the software or data they contain, as this is outside the scope of the book.

Assessing an FTP archive

The generic criteria relating to purpose and coverage discussed in Chapter 3 are applicable to an assessment of FTP archives. The types of software or data available from a site will obviously be a central consideration, and other issues include the format of any software, and whether software for different platforms or types of computer is available. In addition, sites might provide access to upgrades and older versions of data or software, as well as to trial versions of software, and it should be possible easily to distinguish the different file types. The availability of a mirror site is often useful in improving access speeds, and evaluators may wish to compare the coverage and frequency of updating of the mirror site with the original location.

Many of the currency and maintenance issues are also applicable, particularly for those interested in software upgrades. Evaluators may need to know how regularly a site is updated, and whether there is a time delay between software development or data generation and its availability from the site.

Some of the aspects of authority and reputation are applicable. A site may have an excellent reputation as a source of software. For example, an Apple site would obviously be the most authoritative source for Apple Macintosh software. A related issue is the origin of any data or software, and information on this should be available. Many of the accuracy issues are not applicable to FTP archives, but a site may provide some quality-control facilities which could provide a useful filter; it may also certify that all its files have been checked for viruses.

Accessibility, presentation, and arrangement

The Internet is used because it is a fast and convenient means of accessing files and data. Thus the accessibility criteria are important, including whether there is a mirror site to improve access speeds. However, unless an archive is accessed via a WWW site, many of the presentation and arrangement issues are not relevant. Issues which are of concern are the availability of information on file sizes, and the availability of facilities to browse or search materials by filename, platform, or type of application. Other useful features are information on software version numbers and the expiration date for any trial versions.

Ease of use

As with other sources, contact information for a site maintainer is often useful. Help information, perhaps in the form of a README file (usually a text file discussing the contents of the site) or a site FAQ, might be useful, and evaluators should consider the value and usefulness of any such information which is provided. Where a search facility is available, help information will also be useful. Evaluators could also compare an archive with others in order to determine whether it provides unique coverage of software or data, or whether there are any particularly useful features or facilities which assist in file transfer.

EXAMPLE

Evaluating the WinSite archive

The *WinSite* archive (**http://www.winsite.com/**) claims to be the "planet's largest archive for Windows." It is well-known and widely used as a source for Windows software. Indeed, the long list of local mirror sites across the world indicates the level of use (there are eighteen mirror sites in North America alone, with further mirrors in Africa, Asia, Europe, the Middle East, South America, the South Pacific, and the Pacific Rim). Moreover, the availability of this number of mirror sites should ensure that the resource is fast to access from almost anywhere in the world. Obviously anyone interested in using a mirror site would need to compare the coverage and frequency of updating with the original to ensure that the same files are covered, as well as to identify any additional advantages, such as the availability of materials of local relevance.

The archive is accessible through a WWW site, and options from the opening screen include facilities to browse or search the site. Links to special areas include "hot software," "tech area," and "games." Browsing the archive is straightforward – options displayed include "Windows 3.x files," "Windows 95 files," "Windows NT files," "games," and "tech area," indicating the variety of types of software for different platforms. Selecting the "tech area" leads to further options such as "Win95 programming utilities," followed by a list of the files themselves.

Figure 4.8 displays the details of files listed in the *WinSite* archive. As can be seen, many of the details mentioned earlier are listed, including the filename, file size (indicating how long the files are likely to take to download), the date the file was added to the archive, and a description of the file. Therefore, the site is very easy to navigate and use, and valuable information is provided for

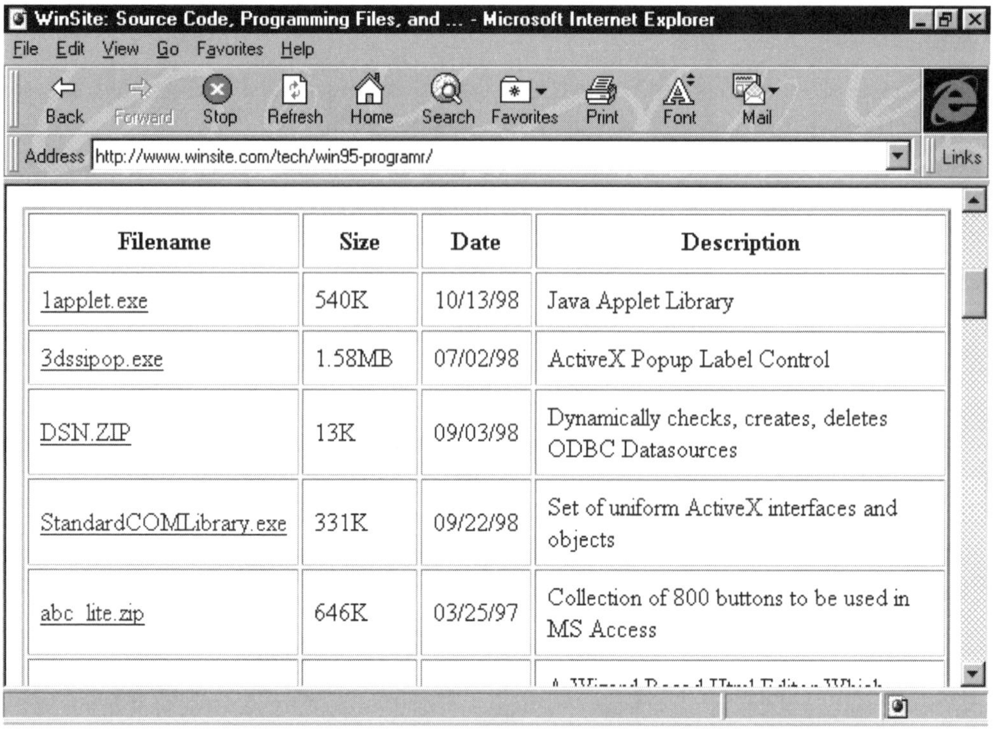

WinSite: Source Code, Programming Files, and ... - Microsoft Internet Explorer

File Edit View Go Favorites Help

Back Forward Stop Refresh Home Search Favorites Print Font Mail

Address http://www.winsite.com/tech/win95-programr/   Links

Filename	Size	Date	Description
1applet.exe	540K	10/13/98	Java Applet Library
3dssipop.exe	1.58MB	07/02/98	ActiveX Popup Label Control
DSN.ZIP	13K	09/03/98	Dynamically checks, creates, deletes ODBC Datasources
StandardCOMLibrary.exe	331K	09/22/98	Set of uniform ActiveX interfaces and objects
abc_lite.zip	646K	03/25/97	Collection of 800 buttons to be used in MS Access

Fig. 4.8 *File details from the WinSite FTP archive. WinSite is produced by Winsite Group Inc.*

the user about the different software which is available. The search facility is also straightforward – the site is searchable by both keyword or filename, and there is an option to specify the platform type. In addition, copyright details and a contact e-mail address are available. There is also extensive help information, links to various Usenet newsgroups such as *comp.os.ms-windows. win95.setup* where issues relating to the software available via the archive are likely to be discussed, as well as FAQs for downloading files, searching the archive, or unzipping files.

An overall impression of this site is that it is an invaluable source for Windows software – a range of different materials is available for different Windows platforms, the archive is likely to be fast from almost anywhere in the world, and it is easy to use and navigate. The providers have also attempted to accommodate the needs of users by offering information on the files which are available, as well as extensive help information and contact details.

CHECKLIST

Assessing FTP archives

☑ Wwhat is the purpose of the archive?

☑ What is the coverage of the archive? What software or data are available? In what formats are the software or data? Are software or data available for different types of computers and platforms? Are upgrades and older versions of data or software available? Are trial versions of software available?

☑ Is the site easily accessible?

☑ Is a mirror site available? What is the coverage of the mirror site in comparison with the original? How frequently is the mirror site updated in comparison with the original?

☑ What is the reputation of the archive? Is it a well-known source for data or software?

☑ Are there any quality-control or virus-checking facilities? Are they effective?

☑ Is the archive well-maintained? Is there a time delay between software development or data generation and its availability via the archive?

☑ Is contact information available for a site maintainer?

☑ Is information available on file origins, software version numbers, the expiration date for trial versions, and file sizes?

☑ Is there a search facility? Does the facility allow users to browse or search by filename, platform, or type of application?

☑ Is the archive easy to use, and are there any user support facilities? Is there any help information, FAQ, or README files? Is there any help information for any search facilities? How useful and valuable is the information provided?

☑ How does the archive compare with other similar archives?

☑ What overall impression of the quality of the archive is created after examining it?

Current awareness services

Current awareness services (CASs) are services which are designed to alert users concerning developments on a particular topic or issue. Various types of CASs are available via the Internet, including WWW sites on the contents of current journals, or mailing lists on sources of funding for those involved in research. Examples already mentioned in Chapter 3 were two job vacancies services available via the WWW, one of which was also available as a mailing list. Essentially, the criteria used will depend upon the format of the service (whether a mailing list or a WWW site) as well as upon the needs of the user.

Assessing Current awareness services

Almost all of the generic criteria discussed in Chapter 3 will be applicable to CASs that are accessible via the WWW. However, issues relating to accessibility, presentation and arrangement, and ease of use are less applicable to services which are available as a mailing list.

As with almost any source of information, evaluators will need to appraise the coverage of the services. One factor in addition to those already discussed in Chapter 3 is whether it is possible to submit a profile to the service in order to restrict the information received to the subjects of most interest. Obviously evaluators would need to appraise the effectiveness of any such facilities, possibly through trial usage if this is possible, or by consulting existing users of the service. In relation to mailing lists, an additional issue is the ability easily to identify the subjects covered by individual postings, for example through the use of conventions for the subject headings of postings. Such facilities can enable users to assess quickly and easily whether they wish to read a posting.

Currency is another area of concern, and evaluators will need to determine the frequency of updating of a site or the frequency of distribution of a mailing list, and the currency of the information which is distributed. A further consideration is the timeliness of the information. Timeliness refers to whether information is received when it is most needed. Considerations include whether journal contents information is received at the same time as publication of the journal itself, and whether job details are received before the closing dates for applications. Cost and any restrictions to access should also be determined, as many CASs charge for their services or require registration.

Again, as with most types of sources, evaluators may also want to compare a CAS with other similar services which are available, and to consider whether one CAS offers any unique services or covers a unique subject area.

EXAMPLE

Evaluating Current awareness services from Elsevier Science

Elsevier Science is a well-known publishing company involved in the production and distribution of various scientific journals. As shown in Figure 4.9, the company offers two alerting and awareness services (**http://www.elsevier.nl/home-page/alert.htt**). The first, "ContentsSearch," provides the tables of contents of over 1,000 *Elsevier Science* journals. Coverage dates back to January 1995, and the tables of contents appear approximately six weeks after publication. Thus, this service could not be used by an individual interested in older journals, and it is also unlikely to be of interest to someone who wants to know the contents of a journal as it is published. However, the service is easy to use and it is a straightforward process to find the contents lists of particular journals – there is a keyword search facility, and it is possible to browse the service by author or journal title.

The second service displayed in Figure 4.9, "ContentsDirect," is an e-mail service which "delivers journal tables of contents directly" to the user's com-

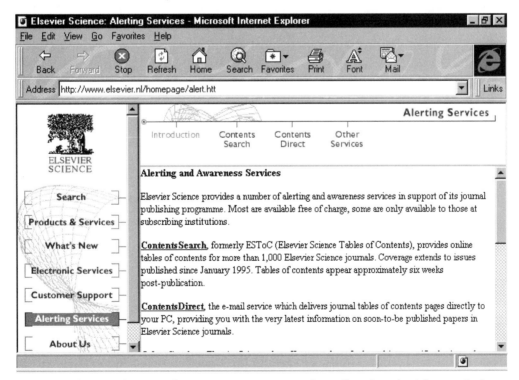

Fig. 4.9 *Elsevier Science Current awareness services. Reprinted with permission from Elsevier Science*

129

puter, providing "the very latest information on soon-to-be published papers in *Elsevier Science* journals." The process of registering to use the service is fairly straightforward: users must complete a registration form and select a username and password; if cookies are enabled on the user's machine, they are then automatically logged into the site. Users can then select the subject areas and the journal titles they are interested in. Surprisingly, this service is free and anyone can select as many journal titles as he or she wishes. The contents listings are then automatically e-mailed to the user regularly – the service sounds excellent for those interested in scientific journals. However, an evaluator would need to subscribe to the service, perhaps for a limited time period, to determine whether the claims for the currency of the postings and the frequency and regularity of updating are accurate.

FAQs

FAQ, pronounced "fack," stands for Frequently Asked Questions. A FAQ is a file of frequently asked questions, with the answers, about a particular topic or issue. FAQs originated from Usenet newsgroups and discussion lists where individuals, often those responsible for the discussion list or newsgroup, develop a file of the most frequently asked questions posted to the group or list. The FAQ is then recommended to newcomers and periodically posted to the newsgroup or discussion list in order to prevent the same questions being asked which have already been discussed exhaustively. However, FAQs are now much more widely used – they are often produced as a source of help information for particular WWW sites or FTP archives, and they are also used as a means of presenting information on a specific subject or issue – the example discussed later in this section is a FAQ for WWW security issues.

Assessing FAQs

Many of the generic criteria discussed in Chapter 3 are applicable to the evaluation of FAQs. Particular considerations are the purpose of the FAQ, the subject area covered, whether the subject has been covered comprehensively, whether there are pointers to further information, the knowledge and expertise of the authors, and the likely accuracy of the information. There is an assumption that FAQs are not authoritative sources of information, partly owing to their origins in Usenet newsgroups. However, this is not necessarily the case – the authority and likely accuracy of the information is dependent upon the knowl-

CHECKLIST

Assessing Current Awareness Services

☑ What is the purpose of the service?

☑ What is the coverage of the service? Is it possible to submit a profile to the service in order to limit the information received to particular subject areas?

☑ What is the reputation and expertise of any organizations involved in the production of the service?

☑ What is the likely accuracy of the information?

☑ Is the information current? How frequently is the service updated or is the mailing list distributed? Is the information provided by the service timely? Is the information provided to the user when it is most needed?

☑ Is the service available as a mailing list, a WWW site, or both?

☑ Is the service easily accessible?

☑ Is the information well-presented and arranged? Is it easy to identify the subjects covered by individual postings for mailing lists?

☑ Is the service easy to use, and are there any user support facilities?

☑ How does the service compare with other similar services?

☑ What overall impression of the quality of the service is created after examining it?

edge and expertise of the author and/or institution involved in the production of the FAQ, and these issues would need to be considered when making a judgment.

The currency of the information should also be determined, although the importance of this will depend upon the nature of the information and whether there is a need for it to be up-to-date (a Star Trek FAQ was mentioned in Chapter 3 which was four years out-of-date, but it is less likely that this information will need to be regularly updated compared with the FAQ discussed below which is concerned with WWW security issues).

Factors associated with accessibility, presentation and arrangement, ease of use, and user support are not usually applicable in the evaluation of FAQs as they tend to be text-based and are commonly presented in a straightforward question-and-answer format. However, readers may want to compare a FAQ with others which are available, to consider the uniqueness of a FAQ, and to make an assessment of its overall quality.

EXAMPLE

Evaluating the World Wide Web Security FAQ

Figure 4.10 displays part of the *World Wide Web Security FAQ* (**http://www.w3.org/Security/Faq/www-security-faq.html#contents**). As can be seen, there are 85 questions pertaining to WWW security issues. Browsing both the questions and the answers indicates the comprehensiveness of coverage of the FAQ and the level of detailed information provided about different issues. There is a last-update date for the FAQ, indicating the currency of the information. In addition, there is an introduction to the FAQ which provides some background

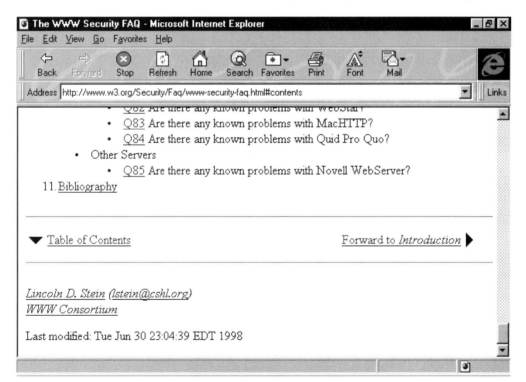

Fig. 4.10 *Details of the World Wide Web Security FAQ*

CHECKLIST

Assessing FAQs

☑ What is the purpose of the FAQ?

☑ What is the coverage of the FAQ? Is the subject covered comprehensively? are there any pointers to further information?

☑ What is the reputation and expertise of any individuals or organizations involved in the production of the FAQ? Is this an authoritative source of information?

☑ What is the likely accuracy of the information?

☑ Is there a last-update date for the FAQ, and is the information current?

☑ Is the FAQ presented in a standard format of questions with links to the answers? Is the information otherwise well-presented and arranged?

☑ How does the FAQ compare with others that are available?

☑ What overall impression of the quality of the FAQ is created after examining it?

information about its purpose, "to answer some of the most frequently asked questions relating to the security implications of running a Web server and using Web browsers." In addition, copyright details are provided and there is an e-mail link to contact the author (shown in Figure 4.10). The FAQ is presented in what has become almost a standard format with the questions listed on the first page and links to the appropriate answers. Users are therefore able to easily browse through the FAQ for the information they require.

Authority

As mentioned above, a major concern with FAQs is the authority of the information and its likely accuracy. The screen shot in Figure 4.10 displays a link to information about the author – Lincoln D. Stein is a researcher who is involved in the development of WWW sites for accessing the human genome. His home page includes numerous links to pages on WWW security, suggesting he is knowledgeable about the topic. There is also a link to the WWW Consortium home page and the address of the FAQ indicates that it is part of the WWW Consortium site (it starts: **http://www.w3.org/**). The WWW Consortium was founded in October 1994 and its work involves the development of protocols and specifications for the WWW. The organization is led by Tim Berners-Lee, the founder of the WWW. This is a very prestigious and highly reputable organization and the location of a FAQ about WWW security issues on the WWW Consortium site itself suggests it is an authoritative (and high-quality) source of information. Moreover, there is a bibliography to published references which adds further weight to the likely accuracy of the information, and the FAQ itself has been published in a book.

References

1. Hernández-Borges, A. A. et al., "Comparative analysis of Pediatric Mailing lists on the Internet," *Pediatrics*, **100** (2), 1997, 1–7.
2. Pedersen, R. C., "A Quantitative Approach to the Description of Internet Mailing Lists," *Serials Librarian,* **30** (1), 1996, 39–47.
3. Anagnostelis, B. and Cooke, A., "Evaluation Criteria for Different Versions of the Same Database: A Comparison of MEDLINE Services Available via the WWW" in *Online '97: Proceedings of the 21st International Online Information Meeting*, 1997, 165–80.

Annotated Bibliography of Sources Related to Evaluating Internet Information

This bibliography is an annotated guide to materials concerned with selection and evaluation strategies. It is intended to provide a guide to further sources of information for those interested in particular aspects of the selection and evaluation of Internet-based information sources. The materials have been listed alphabetically by author.

Alexander, J. and Tate, M., *The Web as a Research Tool: Evaluation Techniques*, [online], 1998. Available: **http://www.science.widener.edu/~withers/evalout.htm** [1999, January 11].

> This page is the textual version of a presentation on the evaluation of materials, and it provides a useful checklist of factors to consider in the evaluation of WWW pages for students. Issues include accuracy, authority, objectivity, currency, and coverage. In addition, the authors consider challenges posed by specific types of materials, such as marketing-oriented WWW pages in which the distinction between advertising and information can become blurred.

Ambre, J. et al., *White Paper: Criteria for Assessing the Quality of Health Information on the Internet* (working draft), [online], 1997. Available: **http://www.mitretek.org/hiti/showcase/documents/criteria.html** [1999, January 11].

> The availability via the Internet of inaccurate and unreliable information within health care and medicine has been an area of special concern and various organizations have developed criteria. The Health Information Technology Institute at Mitretek has devised criteria for assessing the quality of health information available via the Internet. This document, produced by a range of healthcare professionals including consultants and IT specialists, provides an extensive guide to source evaluation intended for consumers of health information. The criteria relate to:

- credibility: source, context, currency, relevance/utility, editorial review process
- content: accuracy, hierarchy of evidence, original sources stated, disclaimer, omissions noted
- disclosure: purpose of site, profiling
- links: selection, architecture, content, back linkages, and descriptions
- design: accessibility, logical organization, internal search engine
- interactivity: mechanism for feedback, chat rooms, tailoring
- caveats: alerts.

Extensive notes, as well as examples, are provided to explain the criteria and offer hints on evaluation. The development of the criteria is an ongoing project and at the time of writing an implementation and testing stage was underway.

Anagnostelis, B. and Cooke, A., "Evaluation Criteria for Different Versions of the Same Database: A Comparison of MEDLINE Services Available via the WWW" in *Online '97: Proceedings of the 21st International Online Information Meeting*, 1997, 165–80.

As mentioned in Chapter 4, during the mid-1990s a number of sites began to offer free access via the Internet to different versions of the MEDLINE database. This paper arose from a recognition of the potential problems associated with the availability of free access to a database which had traditionally been made available through library services. In particular, questions arose regarding which version librarians themselves should use, which version they should recommend to their users, and how they should approach selecting and evaluating the different versions.

The paper compares a range of different versions of the MEDLINE database in order to devise evaluation criteria for assessing different versions of the same database. The databases are compared in terms of their authority, coverage, accessibility, currency, the retrieval mechanism, ease of use, the availability of any unique features, and any help or user support. An appendix to the article summarizes the criteria proposed for evaluating different versions of the same database. This article will appeal to any readers interested in evaluation generally, or more specifically those interested in comparing different versions of the same database.

Argus Clearinghouse Ratings System: How Guides Are Rated, [online]. Available: **http://www.clearinghouse.net/ratings.html** [1999, January 11].

> The *Argus Clearinghouse* (discussed in Chapter 2) selects and evaluates evaluative guides to the Internet. Details are available about the rating process, which addresses the level of resource description and resource evaluation, the guide design and organizational scheme, and the use of metadata. Various additional issues are listed under each heading. Each guide receives between one and five ticks for each aspect of evaluation, and an average number of ticks is calculated for each guide. The document is therefore a useful source, particularly for anyone interested in the process of rating Internet-based materials.

Auer, N., *Bibliography on Evaluating Internet Resources*, [online], 1997. Available: **http://refserver.lib.vt.edu/libinst/critTHINK.HTM** [1999, January 11].

> There has been a vast increase in interest in quality issues relating to information which can be accessed on the Internet, and too many guides to selection and evaluation are now available to describe here. However, numerous authors have begun to collect together available materials, and the bibliography maintained by Auer must be one of the most comprehensive in this area. Other bibliographies are available from Hofman and Worsfold, Smith, and Wilkinson et al. (discussed below).
>
> Auer's list covers over 70 items available in print or on the Internet dealing with information quality assessment. Seven discussion lists are also included. Although no annotation is provided about the different items, this bibliography is a useful guide to available materials.

Blue Web'n Evaluation Rubric, [online], 1997. Available: **http://www.kn.pacbell.com/wired/bluewebn/rubric.html** [1999, January 11].

> The *Blue Web'n* site is a guide to selected and evaluated resources which are intended for educational purposes. The criteria used by the site will therefore be of interest to readers interested in quality issues associated with educational materials. The criteria are listed according to the format of materials (whether materials are user-friendly, aesthetically courteous, or aesthetically appealing), the content (whether materials are credible, useful, rich, or interdisciplinary), and whether materials add to the learning process by challenging learners to think, engaging the learner or integrating different skills.

Brandt, D. Scott., "Evaluating Information on the Internet," *Computers in Libraries*, **16** (5), 1996, 44–6.

> Brandt discusses a range of issues associated with evaluating the quality of information available via the Internet. In particular, he distinguishes between searching for information and evaluating its quality, and suggests assessing the validity, reliability, and authenticity of information, and whether a source is pertinent to a user's needs.

Cassel, R., "Selection Criteria for Internet Resources," *College and Research Libraries News*, **56** (2), 1995, 92–3.

> Following the provision of Internet access, Binghamptom University Library developed guidelines for selecting and evaluating Internet resources. The article briefly describes the selection criteria and will be of particular interest to library and information science professionals who are involved in selecting resources for inclusion in library collections.

Ciolek, T. M. and Goltz, I. M. (eds.), *Information Quality WWW Virtual Library: The Internet Guide to the Construction of Quality Online Resources*, [online]. Available: **http://www.ciolek.com/WWWVL-InfoQuality.html** [1999, January 11].

> The *Information Quality WWW Virtual Library* is an extensive collection of materials relating to different aspects of quality and the Internet. It is an essential starting point for any readers interested in pursuing the topic further, particularly authors of Internet-based materials who are interested in quality in the design and maintenance of their own materials. Resources include:
>
> - building quality WWW resources (design, development, and administration of WWW sites and materials)
> - building quality non-WWW resources (FTP, Telnet, databases, mailing lists)
> - quality information systems: catalog of potent truisms ("self-evident truths")
> - evaluation of information sources (maintained by Alistair Smith and described below)
> - "top 10 ways to make your WWW service a flop"
> - information quality definitions
> - user interface design issues.

Collins, B. R., "Beyond Cruising: Reviewing," *Library Journal*, **121** (3), 1996, 122–4.

> Collins considers the role of librarians and other information professionals in selecting and evaluating sources available via the Internet and briefly considers criteria relating to the content, authority, currency, organization, and accessibility of a source, as well as the availability of search facilities.

Demas, S. et al., "The Internet and Collection Development: Mainstreaming Selection of Internet Resources," *Library Resources and Technical Services*, **39** (3), 1995, 275–90.

> The authors describe the results of their work on tailoring traditional collection development policies to accommodate Internet-based sources. The article considers the challenges to collection development posed by the availability of material via networks, and collection development issues in relation to the electronic library. A taxonomy of Internet materials is provided, with details of the collection development policy developed by the authors. Again, this article will be of particular interest to the library profession.

Edwards, J., "The Good, the Bad and the Useless: Evaluating Internet Resources," *Ariadne*, **16**, 1998 [online]. Available: **http://www.ariadne.ac.uk/ issue16/digital** [1999, January 11].

> This paper provides a brief general overview of different quality issues relating to the evaluation of Internet resources. The author considers questions relating to access (e.g., stability of the site, hardware and software specifications), quality (responsibility for the site and quality of content), and ease of use (ease of navigation, availability of site map, etc.). The article includes links to collection development policies for electronic materials, bibliographies on evaluation, and guides to evaluating Internet-based materials.

Evaluating Internet Resources for SOSIG, [online], 1998. Available: **http://sosig. ac.uk/desire/ecrit.html** [1999, January 11].

> The *Social Sciences Information Gateway* (*SOSIG*), described in Chapter 2, is a gateway to high-quality materials within the social sciences which are available via the Internet. *SOSIG* is one of the subject-based gateways developed under the *eLib* program. The above document lists the criteria used by developers of the service for selecting and evaluating materials. The criteria are divided into content (validity, authority and reputation,

substantiveness, accuracy, comprehensiveness, uniqueness, composition, and organization), form (ease of navigation, provision of user support, use of recognized standards, appropriate use of technology, aesthetics), and process (information integrity, site integrity, and system integrity). The document provides a useful guide to source assessment, particularly for social science materials.

Grassian, E., *Thinking Critically about World Wide Web Resources*, [online], 1997. Available: **http://www.library.ucla.edu/libraries/college/instruct/web/critical.htm** [1999, January 11].

Grassian offers a checklist of criteria relating to evaluation of aspects such as audience, purpose, accuracy, comprehensiveness, the value of the information provided, the authority or expertise of the individual or group concerned, and whether the site follows good graphic-design principles.

Harris, R., *Evaluating Internet Research Sources* [online], 1997. Available: **http://www.sccu.edu/faculty/R_Harris/evalu8it.htm** [1999, January 11].

Harris covers a range of issues relating to research sources available via the Internet. He first proposes a preevaluation, whereby users consider what exactly they are looking for. He then suggests selecting resources by considering, for example, which types of materials are most likely to be reliable. The author proposes a CARS (credibility, accuracy, reasonableness, and support) checklist for assessing the quality of sources. Within these areas of assessment, the criteria include:

- the author's credentials
- evidence of quality control
- indicators of a lack of credibility
- timeliness
- comprehensiveness
- audience and purpose
- fairness
- objectivity
- moderateness
- consistency
- source of documentation or bibliography
- corroboration
- external consistency.

Various examples and explanatory notes are provided, making this a useful guide for Internet users who are interested in evaluating research materials.

Hernández-Borges, A. A. et al., "Comparative Analysis of Pediatric Mailing Lists on the Internet," *Pediatrics*, **100** (2), 1997, 1–7.

As discussed in Chapter 4 under "Assessing Usenet Newsgroups and Discussion Lists," Hernández-Borges et al. have developed a quantitative technique for evaluating the potential quality of a range of pediatric mailing lists. In order to devise the method, MEDLINE was searched for the names of mailing list subscribers and an impact factor was calculated for each of the subscribers' papers using the *Science Citation Index*. An average impact factor was calculated for each list, as well as an average impact factor per participant and per message to the group. An average number of postings per author was also calculated. The results indicated, for example, the most popular and active list, and the list with the highest quality per posting.

The authors propose that the methodology offers a technique for assessing the quality of mailing lists because it is "based on the accumulation of defined impact factors generated by published articles of the various members of the discussion groups, a way for any scientific group to gain prestige in a given field of science." The methodology is not necessarily restricted to this discipline, although it is only likely to be of relevance to those concerned with evaluating lists with an academic focus. While it would require extensive time and effort to evaluate a discussion list using this methodology, the article will be of interest to those seeking more information on the evaluation of discussion lists in particular.

Hinchliffe, L. J., *Resource Selection and Information Evaluation*, [online], 1997. Available: **http://alexia.lis.uiuc.edu/~janicke/Evaluate.html** [1999, January 11].

Hinchliffe proposes criteria for the evaluation of information available via the Internet in relation to format, scope, comparison to other sources, authority, treatment, arrangement, and cost. The criteria are each discussed briefly.

Hofman, P. and Worsfold, E., *Selection Criteria for Quality Controlled Information Gateways*, [online], 1997. Available: **http://www.ukoln.ac.uk/metadata/ DESIRE/quality/** [1999, January 11].

Hofman and Worsfold examined the various methods and criteria used by a range of different subject-based information gateways and virtual libraries for selecting and evaluating materials in order to develop:

- a generalized graphical model of a functioning subject gateway that would enable a systematic approach to quality issues in the provision, development, control, monitoring, and analysis of a subject gateway
- a structured list of selection criteria that could be used as a reference tool by subject gateways and enable new and evolving subject gateways to produce their own tailored selection schemes without having to reinvent wheels.

In order to develop the criteria, a list of 250 quality indicators was collected by examining those used by existing subject-based gateway services and by other Internet services, and those described in the literature. Following the removal of duplicates, the standardization of the language, and a qualitative analysis to group the criteria thematically, a second list of criteria was developed and evaluated.

The criteria are divided into five groups:

- scope criteria: considering the users
- content criteria: evaluating the content
- form criteria: evaluating the medium
- process criteria: evaluating the system
- collection management criteria: considering the service.

The development of the criteria is discussed in detail and the criteria have been developed into a reference tool, which is included as an appendix, along with an appendix of definitions of quality, the selection criteria used by a range of gateway services, and an extensive bibliography of material relating to quality assessment.

The authors are based at the Institute for Learning and Research Technology at the University of Bristol in the UK, and have also been involved in the development of the *Internet Detective* (discussed below).

Internet Detective, [online]. Available: **http://www.sosig.ac.uk/desire/internet-detective.html** [1999, January 11].

The *Internet Detective* is an electronic toolkit designed to enable users to learn about evaluating Internet-based sources of information. This is a fairly informal but extensive and valuable resource which aims to enable users to:

- be aware of the key factors that affect the quality of Internet information
- learn practical hints and tips for evaluating the quality of an Internet resource
- see a comprehensive set of quality criteria
- see practical examples of the evaluation process
- try out the process for themselves on a sample of Internet resources.

The *Internet Detective* includes practical "hints and tips" and interactive quizzes. There are three worked examples, which include relevant evaluative questions, where to look to make an assessment, and an overall evaluation of three resources.

The authors of the *Internet Detective* are based at the Institute for Learning and Research Technology at the University of Bristol in the UK and the project was funded by the European Union as part of the *Telematics for Research Program*. The toolkit is aimed at any Internet user but it will be of particular value to library professionals, researchers, teachers, and students. The *Internet Detective* is freely available, although users must register to use it; after registering and logging on, users are automatically taken to the last point they had reached in the package.

Jones, D., *Critical Thinking in an Online World*, [online], 1996. Available: **http://www.library.ucsb.edu/untangle/jones.html** [1999, January 11].

With the development of the Internet, and the ease with which information can be disseminated via the WWW in particular, librarians and other information professionals have become increasingly involved in training library users in critical thinking skills. This article discusses some of the ideas behind critical thinking, and situations in which teaching critical thinking skills is appropriate. A package designed to teach critical thinking is also outlined. The article provides some useful background, but readers are also recommended to refer to the article by Tate and Alexander (see p. 150) which provides a more detailed guide to the factors for consideration in critical thinking.

Kovacs, D. K. et al., "A Model for Planning and Providing Reference Services Using Internet Resources," *Library Trends*, **42** (4), 1994, 638–47.

> This article discusses the role of library and information professionals in relation to the provision of reference services using Internet-based materials. The following are considered: information skills, awareness of information services and resources, information retrieval, and information management. The evaluation of information sources is briefly considered.

Lycos Top 5% Ratings, [online], 1998. Available: **http://www.lycos.com/help/top5-help2.html** [1999, January 11].

> As discussed in Chapter 2, a number of rating and reviewing services were developed during the mid-1990s with a view to providing more effective access to Internet-based materials. Many provide very little or no information about their selection policies. However, the *Lycos Top 5%* service (described further in Chapter 2) includes details on its approach to selection as part of its help information. Sites are evaluated according to three rating categories: content, design, and overall assessment; sites are then awarded a score for each category. The average score is defined in relation to "classic rock bands." For example, sites rating between 90 and 100 are comparable to "the Beatles, Rolling Stones, Bob Dylan . . . not only good but important and influential. Sites that signal a leading trend on the Internet," while sites scoring between one and 40 are of "unusually low quality," and have no band associated with them. The criteria used by the *Lycos Top 5%* service are obviously less formal than those described in this book. However, they have been included here for readers interested in informal approaches to assessing sources.

McLachlan, K., *WWW CyberGuide Ratings for Content Evaluation*, [online], 1996. Available: **http://www.cyberbee.com/guides.html** [1999, January 11].

> McLachlan has developed two rating forms: one for the evaluation of content and one for the evaluation of WWW site design. Both are intended for use by teachers and students in evaluating the quality of WWW sites. The criteria include:

- speed
- first impressions
- ease of navigation
- use of graphics, sound, and video

- content and information
- currency
- availability of further information.

Under each criterion, a series of statements is listed with a rating scale from one to five, where one equates with "poor," and five with "excellent." The use of graphics, sound, and videos, for example, is assessed by allocating a score from one to five for the following statements:

- the graphics/sounds/videos are clearly labeled, clearly identified
- the graphics/sounds/videos serve a clear purpose, appropriate for my intended audience
- the graphics/sounds/videos will aid my students in reaching the desired objectives for this site.

A total number of points is then calculated for each site to determine its overall rating.

While there is no explanatory information about the content of the form, the form itself is clearly laid out, and could be easily adapted to suit the needs of others requiring a similar means for evaluating sources numerically.

Medical Matrix: About Medical Matrix: Ranking System, [online], 1997. Available: **http://www.medmatrix.org/info/about.html** [1999, January 11].

Medical Matrix is "a large, peer-reviewed, annotated database of Internet clinical resources." Sites are evaluated by practising healthcare professionals and periodically reviewed by an editorial board drawn from members of the American Medical Informatics Association. The service provides details of the procedures used for evaluating and ranking resources for inclusion in the database. Materials are evaluated and ranked according to:

- peer review: previously evaluated, verifiable, endorsed, dated, current, referenced (1–20 points)
- application: ability to enhance the knowledge database of the primary care clinician or specialist at the point of care (1–10 points)
- media: text, hypertext, or use of multimedia (images, video, sound) in the context of the resource (e.g., image database) (1–5 points)
- feel: search features, navigation tools, composition, advanced HTML tools, and integration within a larger database (1–5 points)

- ease of access: clinical content highlighted, reliability and speed of the link, bytes to the page (1–5 points)
- dimension: size, effort, and importance to the discipline (1–5 points).

The rankings are used to assign 1–5 stars according to the following guidelines:

- specialized knowledge with suitable clinical content (no stars)
- suitable clinical content, well-authored, and maintained (one star)
- a valuable resource for improving general knowledge in the discipline, or other outstanding features such as multimedia (two stars)
- one of the best of a speciality category/subcategory and a valuable place to go (three stars)
- an outstanding site across all categories and a premier Web page for the discipline (four stars)
- an award-winning site for the medical Internet (five stars).

This document will be of particular interest to individuals interested in assessing the likely value and usefulness of Internet-based resources which are of interest to health care and medical practice.

OMNI Guidelines for Resource Evaluation, [online], 1997. Available: **http://omni.ac.uk/agec/evalguide.html** [1999, January 11].

Organizing Medical Networked Information (OMNI), is one of the subject-based information gateways developed as part of the eLib program (described in Chapter 2). Librarians, information professionals, and subject experts are involved in the identification, selection, evaluation, and description of resources, and the *OMNI* project has developed detailed *Guidelines for Resource Evaluation*, which are designed to assist in formalizing the evaluation process. The guidelines are of interest, not only to readers concerned with the identification of resources for inclusion in gateway services, but also to those involved in the evaluation of resources generally, and of health-related and biomedical materials in particular.

The guidelines specify key selection principles, namely an initial consideration of whether material contains "substantive information of relevance to the OMNI user community," thus excluding personal home pages, collections of links, material which is strictly local in context, and advertisements. The remaining guidelines are then divided into contextual issues (scope, audience, authority, and provenance), content evaluation (coverage, accuracy, currency, and uniqueness), and access evaluation (accessibility, design, and layout). The areas of evaluation are explained and questions requiring consideration are clearly listed.

Payton, T., *Evaluation Rubrics for Web Sites*, [online], 1998. Available: **http://seic.k12.in.us/~west/edu/evaltr.htm** [1999, January 11].

This site provides rating forms, with criteria and rating scales, for the evaluation of WWW sites for primary grades, intermediate grades, and secondary grades. The rating form for primary grades covers issues such as design, content, technical elements, and credibility of materials. Evaluators can rate each site on a scale of one (poor) to five (excellent) for each criterion, totalling up to 25 points for each site. Similar aspects are covered for intermediate and secondary grades, but greater details are provided under each criterion, enabling a more comprehensive evaluation of the sites.

Pedersen, R. C., "A Quantitative Approach to the Description of Internet Mailing Lists," *Serials Librarian*, 30 (1), 1996, 39–47.

As discussed in Chapter 4 under "Assessing Usenet newsgroups and discussion lists," Pedersen describes a study to develop a quantitative technique for determining whether mailing lists are likely to meet subscribers' needs. In order to evaluate mailing lists, the author proposes calculating the average number of messages per day posted to the list, and categorizing the messages according to their content, such as whether they are administrative, announcements, discussion, pointers to further information, etc. He then suggests group characteristics can be summarized according to the volume of postings and the nature of the messages. For example, Pedersen describes one group he evaluated using the technique as having "very light traffic consisting entirely of announcements," while another was "a more active forum . . . dominated by relevant discussion" and "a good source of job announcements." As with the methodology proposed by Hernández-Borges et al., this approach would require time and effort to implement, but will be of interest to those seeking more information on the evaluation of discussion lists in particular.

Pratt, G. F. et al., "Guidelines for Internet Resource Selection," *College and Research Libraries News*, 1996, 134–5.

Brief guidelines for the selection and evaluation of information sources available via the Internet are provided under the following headings:

- quality and content
- relevancy

- ease of use
- reliability and stability
- cost and copyright
- hardware and software.

The guidelines are provided in the format of a checklist.

Rettig, J., *Beyond "Cool": Analog Models for Reviewing Digital Resources*, [Online], 1996. Available: **http://www.onlineinc.com/onlinemag/SeptOL/rettig9.html** [1999, January 11].

> Rettig examines the evaluation criteria used by a range of rating and reviewing services, including *Lycos Top 5%*, to assess materials. The author suggests that the criteria are inappropriate to an evaluation of quality and offer little more than an assessment of the "coolness" of the sites which are evaluated. He therefore discusses the criteria traditionally used by library and other information professionals for assessing reference works, and considers their modification and application to Internet-based materials. Those considered applicable to both WWW sites and reference books include accuracy, appropriateness, authority, completeness, documentation, illustrations, revisions, and ease of use.

SantaVicca, E. F., "Evaluating Internet Resources: The Internet as a Reference and Research Tool: A Model for Educators" in Kinder, R. (ed.), *Librarians on the Internet: Impact on Reference Services*, New York, Hawthorn Press, 1994, 225–36.

> The article briefly discusses the use of the Internet for reference and research purposes, then considers the evaluation of traditional information sources and compares this to the evaluation of Internet sources.

Scholz-Crane, A., *Evaluating World-Wide Web Information*, [online], 1997. Available: **http://crab.rutgers.edu/~scholzcr/eval.html** [1999, January 11].

> Scholz-Crane offers some limited guidance on where to look for evaluative information. She suggests examining the header, body, and footer of a WWW document to determine the author, sponsoring institution, institution, date of creation or revision, intended audience, and purpose of the information. Scholz-Crane also recommends criteria relating to the experience of the author, the potential for bias, when information was last updated, and the intended purpose of the information. A checklist is included for the evaluation of WWW pages.

Smith, A., *Evaluation of Information Sources*, [online], 1998. Available: **http://www.vuw.ac.nz/~agsmith/evaln/evaln.htm** [1999, January 11].

> As has already been mentioned before, there has been an increase in interest in quality issues relating to information which can be accessed via the Internet, and too many guides to selection and evaluation are now available to be described here. Like Auer (see p. 137), Smith has attempted to collect materials relating to the evaluation of information sources, and includes pointers to the criteria used by a number of different gateway services, as well as links to commentaries on the evaluation process. Again, this is a useful starting point for those interested in examining any further materials.

Smith, A., "Testing the Surf: Criteria for Evaluating Internet Information Resources," *Public Access Computer Systems Review*, [online], 8 (3), 1997. Available: **http://info.lib.uh.edu/pr/v8/n3/smit8n3.html** [1999, January 11].

> Smith examines criteria for the evaluation of paper-based sources of information and provides a review of materials relating to selection and evaluation. He suggests a "toolbox" of evaluation criteria:

- scope
- content (including accuracy, authority, currency, uniqueness, links made to other resources, quality of writing)
- graphic and multimedia design
- purpose and audience
- workability (including user-friendliness, required computing environment, search facilities, browsability, organization, interactivity, and connectivity)
- cost.

Various questions are listed in relation to the assessment of each criterion. In addition, Smith provides a useful table which compares the criteria used in the assessment of sources by different subject-based gateways, virtual libraries, and rating and reviewing services. The article includes a useful bibliography as well as descriptions of the various gateway and reviewing services.

Starr, S. S., "Evaluating Physical Science Reference Sources on the Internet," in Kinder, R. (ed.), *Librarians on the Internet: Impact on Reference Services*, New York, Hawthorn Press, 1994, 261–73.

> This article classifies and reviews a sample of physical science materials available via the Internet and proposes criteria for evaluation. Materials are categorized into bibliographies, indexes and abstracts, handbooks, manuals and guides, and directories. The proposed criteria are purpose, authority, scope, audience, and format. The criteria are briefly discussed and explained.

Stoker, D. and Cooke, A., "Evaluation of Networked Information Sources," in Helal, A. H. and Weiss, J. W. (eds.), *Information Superhighway: The Role of Librarians, Information Scientists and Intermediaries: Proceedings of the 17th International Essen Symposium 24th–27th October 1994*, Essen, Essen University Library, 1995, 287–312.

> This article assesses the applicability of traditional criteria used by librarians and other information professionals for evaluating reference works to information available via the Internet. The authors discuss the following criteria:

- authority
- genealogy
- scope and treatment (including purpose, coverage, currency, methods of revision, accuracy, objectivity, and audience)
- format
- arrangement
- technical considerations
- price
- availability
- user support.

Tate, M. and Alexander, J., "Teaching Critical Evaluation Skills for World-Wide Web Resources," *Computers in Libraries*, 1996, 49–55.

> As already mentioned (see Jones p. 143), there has been an increase in material relating to the teaching of critical thinking skills for library users. Tate and Alexander describe a course developed for teaching critical thinking, which is a particularly good example of the issues requiring consideration in the development of any such course. The criteria used for source assessment (accuracy, authority, objectivity, currency, and coverage) are

discussed, together with examples of both high-quality and low-quality WWW pages, and consideration of certain peculiar types and aspects of material:

- marketing-oriented WWW pages
- pages blending entertainment, information, and advertising
- hypertext links
- software requirements
- search engine retrieval
- instability of WWW sites
- susceptibility to alteration.

Specific types of pages (namely advocacy, business/marketing, informational, news, and personal) are briefly discussed, and a clearly presented checklist is provided which includes points to consider when examining an informational page. This is a helpful and practical guide for any individuals interested in developing their own materials for teaching critical thinking or for those interested in pursuing the topic further.

Tillman, H. N., *Evaluating Quality on the Net*, [online], 1997. Available: **http://www.tiac.net/users/hope/findqual.html** [1999, January 11].

This document is the transcript of a paper presented in November 1997. The paper examines the relevance of existing criteria to information available on the Internet, and discusses a wide range of tools which seek to provide selective access to resources. The author proposes a checklist of key indicators of quality, including the ease of finding sites, the ease of identifying authority and currency, the stability of the information, and ease of use in terms of convenience, organization, and speed of access. The author also provides "advice for those publishing, promoting or communicating via the Net."

Wilkinson, G. L. et al., *Evaluating the Quality of Internet Information Sources*, [online], 1997. Available: **http://itech1.coe.uga.edu/Faculty/gwilkinson/webeval.html** [1999, January 11].

A research project based at the University of Georgia has attempted to identify and rate the importance of various criteria to develop a generic evaluation tool. A range of sources were consulted to identify possible evaluation criteria, including periodicals, journals, online rating services, and authorities on library reference materials. A total of 509 possible criteria or "indicators of quality" were identified. Content analysis was conducted to eliminate duplicate items, to clarify those with ambiguous meaning, and to eliminate meaningless items, such as "I pick the good stuff." The original list was reduced to 125 indicators, which were categorized under eleven headings:

- site access and usability
- resource identification and documentation
- author identification
- authority of author
- information structure and design
- relevance and scope of content
- validity of content
- accuracy and balance of content
- navigation within document
- quality of the links
- aesthetic and affective aspects.

A review panel was selected and asked to identify the focus and importance of each indicator. The indicators were then rated using a six-point scale ranging from one (irrelevant) through to six (essential). The various papers available from this site describe the research in greater detail, list the full set of quality indicators, and list the indicators as ranked by the review panel. Thus, the site is a useful guide to the relative importance of different criteria as assessed by the review panel. An extensive bibliography is also available of material relating to the evaluation of information sources available on the Internet, some of which have not been mentioned here.

Wyatt, J. C., "Commentary: Measuring Quality and Impact of the World-Wide Web," *British Medical Journal*, **314** (7098), 1998 [online]. Available: **http://www.bmj.com/archive/7098ip2.htm** [1999, January 11].

Wyatt provides a table of aspects of a WWW site which might be considered when evaluating reliability. The evaluation aspects are:

- credibility and conflicts of interest
- structure and content of website
- functions of website
- impact of website.

Glossary

Acrobat Reader   The software required for displaying or printing documents in Portable Document Format.

badges   Used here to refer to a small image or icon which can be displayed by a site to indicate that a rating or reviewing service has evaluated it and considered it worth awarding the badge; the *Lycos Top 5%* (discussed in Chapter 2) awards such badges to indicate sites that are part of the "top 5%" of the Internet.

bibliographical database   A database of references to journal articles, books, conference proceedings, etc.

browser   A program which is used to view information available via networks; examples are *Netscape Navigator* and *Internet Explorer* which are browsers used for examining information available via the WWW.

CAL materials *see* Computer Assisted Learning materials.

CAS *see* Current awareness service.

client   Refers to a local computer, and also to the software which resides on a local computer; the user inputs data into the client software which then interprets any data received from a remote computer (the server).

command-line interface (CLI)   An interface which generally appears as a prompt on the screen at which users must type in predefined commands in order to run programs.

Computer Assisted Learning (CAL) materials   Multimedia materials which are designed to aid teaching and learning through the use of computing technology

cookies   A facility which allows users to specify preferences for viewing particular WWW pages; the preferences are saved as a cookie on the user's machine, and each time the user views a page or site, the browser checks to see if the user has any preferences (or cookies) for that page or site; an example of their use is to store usernames and passwords.

counter Used to indicate how many people have visited a site during a specified time-period, and therefore to indicate a site's popularity.

Current awareness service (CAS) A service designed to alert users to new developments in a particular topic or issue; an example is a service which distributes the contents listings of journals.

database A collection of records, each with details of a different data item, whether numeric, textual, or image-based; usually searchable.

discussion list Also sometimes called a "mailing list" or "listserv," a discussion list is circulated to a group of e-mail users who are interested in a particular topic area; e-mail users subscribe to the list, and can then post to it and receive all the messages which are posted.

distributed client–server computing The technology whereby data is located on a remote computer, the server, which is accessible via a network; the software for accessing the data is located on the user's own machine, the client.

electronic journal A journal which is produced in an electronic format; sometimes the electronic equivalent of a paper-based journal, although an increasing number of journals are produced entirely in an electronic format.

eLib The *Electronic Libraries Programme*, a program of nationally funded research projects in the UK which are concerned with the development, implementation and evaluation of the electronic library.

e-mail Electronic mail, software which enables messages to be sent from one person's computer to another across a network or the Internet.

FAQ *see* Frequently Asked Questions.

File Transfer Protocol (FTP) The protocol which enables users to transfer files from one computer to another across a network or the Internet.

frames A facility which is used to divide an HTML page into two or more pages, so that more than one page can be viewed at the same time.

Frequently Asked Questions (FAQ) A file of commonly asked questions, with answers, about a particular topic or issue; these are often used to summarize the most frequently asked questions to a Usenet newsgroup or discussion list, but are also commonly used as a source of help information about WWW sites and pages.

FTP *see* File Transfer Protocol.

FTP archive   A collection of files, such as software, textual materials, or numerical data, which can be accessed and retrieved using FTP *see* File Transfer Protocol.

Gopher   An early example of a distributed client–server tool which presented information available via the Internet through a browsable system of menus; a Gopher browser was required to access the information.

graphical user interface (GUI)   An interface which includes images as well as text which the user can select in order to access information; it can also include browsable menus or boxes into which the user types search terms.

hardware   The tangible parts of a computer, i.e., the system box, screen, keyboard, and other peripherals.

home page   The opening page of any site on the WWW is generally referred to as the "home page"; for example, the first page of an organization's site is the "home page"; an individual's personal site or page is also referred to as a personal home page.

HTML *see* HyperText Mark-up Language.

HTTP *see* HyperText Transfer Protocol.

hypertext   Text which contains cross-references or links (hypertext links) to different parts of the same page or to different pages; information can be browsed by simply clicking on the links.

HyperText Markup Language (HTML)   The language which is used to produce information in a format suitable for dissemination via the WWW.

HyperText Transfer Protocol (HTTP)   One of the standards used to transfer information via the WWW.

interface   The means by which the user communicates with the computer; in particular, what is displayed on the screen to the user; *see also* command-line interface, graphical user interface.

image-based information   Images which are used as a source of information.

Internet   A worldwide network of interconnected networks, connected together using recognized standards to enable electronic communication and the exchange of information.

Internet Explorer   A multimedia browser for accessing information which is available via the WWW.

Java   A programming language which allows an author to create applets, small programs that run within a WWW page.

metadata   Data about data, similar to a bibliographical record, which is written into the HTML of a WWW page itself; it can be used to specify information about a page, such as a description or subject keywords which represent the contents of a site.

meta-search engines   Also sometimes called "meta-crawlers" and "multi-search engines," these allow users to search several search facilities at once.

mirror site   A copy of an original site which is located elsewhere; these contain the same or similar information to the original site and are used to improve access speeds to heavily used sites.

Mosaic   One of the earliest multimedia browsers for accessing the WWW; now largely superseded by *Netscape Navigator* and *Internet Explorer*.

multimedia   Something which encompasses a range of different types of media, such as images, sound, and video clips, as well as text.

multimedia browser   A browser which allows the user to view text, graphics, moving images, etc.

Netscape Navigator   A multimedia browser for accessing information which is available via the WWW; often simply called *Netscape*.

newsgroups *see* Usenet newsgroups

organizational WWW site   A collection of WWW pages that are created and maintained by a particular organization; the opening page is generally referred to as the home page; organizational sites often include subject-based pages and personal home pages.

password   A secret and unique identifier which individuals use, in conjunction with their username, which allows them to log onto a machine or to log into a particular service.

PDF *see* Portable Document Format.

personal home page   A WWW page (or collection of pages) which is maintained by an individual and which relates to his or her personal interests; personal home pages might also include subject-based pages, and are often part of an organizational site.

Portable Document Format (PDF)   A file format created by Adobe Systems, which allows the display or printing of materials in a format which is virtually identical to that of an original paper-based publication; commonly used to present journal articles as they appear on paper; it requires the use of an Acrobat Reader.

protocol A set of data-exchange rules which specify how computers transmit data between different computers and across networks.

query input box The blank box presented on a screen into which users type their search terms or query.

rating and reviewing sites Services which rate and review materials available via the WWW and which are designed for popular appeal; these tend to be informal and use a combination of two of the following: a numerical scoring system, star ratings, brief reviews, and badges; these are designed to indicate the quality of a site or page at a glance, but, as discussed in Chapter 2, it is questionable whether they achieve this.

search engine Software that allows users to search an automatically generated database of WWW materials.

search facility In this context, any tool or facility which can be used to search information which is accessible via the Internet; this includes search engines, subject catalogs and directories, popular rating and reviewing sites, subject-based gateways and virtual libraries, and meta-search engines.

server A remote computer which is accessed by a client via a network.

software Any program which runs on a computer; examples include browsers, e-mail packages, and word processors.

subject-based gateway services A collection of searchable (and usually browsable) resource descriptions which have been developed by library professionals and/or subject experts with the explicit aim of providing access to high-quality sources of information – the descriptions relate only to high-quality materials available via the Internet within a particular subject area.

subject-based pages Pages, and sometimes whole sites, with a particular subject focus.

subject catalog Subject catalogs and directories are search services which involve human input in identifying relevant resources and allocating them to particular subject categories; the tools are usually searchable and browsable via the subject categories; resources are not evaluated by quality prior to inclusion in the catalog or directory.

subject directory *see* subject catalog.

TCP/IP *see* Transmission Control Protocol/Internet Protocol

Telnet   A protocol and application which allows a user to log onto and access or search a remote computer; Telnet is widely used to access remote library catalogs.

text-based browser   A browser which only allows the user to view text; different software must be used to access graphics, moving images, or sound.

thumbnail image   A small-scale image which can be selected in order to view a much larger version of the same image.

tilde   The character "~," which is used in the address of some WWW pages.

Transmission Control Protocol/Internet Protocol (TCIP/IP)   A set of computer networking standards upon which the running of the Internet is based.

Uniform Resource Locator (URL)   The full address of a resource on the Internet; every site or page on the Internet has a unique URL which consists of the protocol (e.g., http), the server name, the domain name, and the pathname of the resource.

Usenet newsgroups   A worldwide distributed system of bulletin boards which are hierarchically arranged into topic areas; these are similar to discussion lists in that users can discuss a particular area of interest, but users do not have to subscribe, and anyone can view the messages (provided they have access to the software required).

username   The name which individuals use to log onto a machine or to log into a particular service; usually individuals will also have a password which is used in conjunction with the username.

virtual libraries   Collections of resources which have been selected, evaluated, and described by library professionals and/or subject experts with the explicit aim of providing access to high-quality sources of information.

World Wide Web (WWW)   The part of the Internet based around HTML documents; hypertext links enable users to move between different parts of the same document, as well as to different documents in different locations.

WWW page   An individual HTML page which is available via the WWW; a collection of related pages is usually referred to as a WWW site.

WWW site   A collection of linked HTML pages available via the WWW generally owned or produced by a single institution or individual.

Index